OU
HANDBOOK

THE OUTDOORS HANDBOOK

Eddie McGee

*Illustrated by Rodney Paull
and Mike Gordon*

BEAVER BOOKS

A Beaver Book
Published by Arrow Books Limited
62–5 Chandos Place, London WC2N 4NW

An imprint of Century Hutchinson Ltd

London Melbourne Sydney Auckland
Johannesburg and agencies throughout the world

First published 1989

Set in Century Schoolbook
by JH Graphics Ltd, Reading

Made and printed in Great Britain
by Courier International Limited
Tiptree, Essex

ISBN 0 09 966190 X

Contents

Introduction

If you feel you are ready to try an outdoor adventure such as a hiking or camping trip without close adult supervision, then I can help. This book covers all you need to know for your first trip; route planning, buying and choosing equipment, basic map reading, first aid, and dealing with emergencies, plus lots of useful tips and advice on survival.

There's lots to do in the countryside. I've included a section on tracking, and ideas on other outdoor pursuits – canoeing, sailing, climbing, or horseback riding – for those of you who want to try something a little more adventurous at a later date.

The countryside is there for all of us to enjoy. With the confidence you'll get from good preparation and carefully chosen equipment, you will be able to enjoy it to the full. Be careful, stay safe, but, above all, have a good time.

1

Planning and preparation

We have all seen TV documentaries and films showing famous explorers pushing their way through dense tropical forest, plodding across vast deserts or snow plains, but have you ever stopped to think how much preparation and planning went into such adventures, sometimes two or three years before everything is finalized.

What people tend to overlook is that any expedition, no matter how small, be it a one-day hiking holiday or a four-month safari, can be very demanding both physically and mentally, and good preparation is absolutely essential. Only a fool sets off on a trip without first ensuring that he or she has all the equipment necessary for safety and survival, and, just as important, a detailed plan of the journey. Every year hundreds of people set out on their first adventure badly prepared, and, sadly, many end up injured, or die tragically when, had they done a little

preparatory work beforehand, they probably
would have lived.

Yes, I'm trying to scare you! But I'm not trying
to scare you off a *properly planned* trip. If you are
well prepared, then you will have a great time,
and nothing will worry you, because you know
you are equipped to cope with even the most
unlikely emergency.

So, let's get down to the nitty gritty. Let's say you
would like to go on a day's hike in the countryside
with a friend. You've mulled the idea over, and
now it's time to think really hard about your
scheme.

Safety in numbers

Be sure to choose a good friend to travel with. It
should be someone you know well, perhaps a
brother/sister or school friend, someone who
shares similar interests and who, like you, wants
to try a little adventure.

Choosing a suitable partner is just as important
as your planning and preparation. You must
ensure that you both get along well. It is a good
idea if your partner is in your own age group, and
has had a little outdoor experience, perhaps
camping out in the back garden. Right from the
start you must both be fully aware of each other's
potential and avoid any misunderstandings.

Away from the familiarity of local landmarks
things can be so different, especially when you
travel far afield. Remember, once you leave the
safety of your home any decisions will have to be

made by you and your travelling companion, so it is important that you get on well together and trust each other's judgement.

Taking the first step

Before you make any list, purchase any clothing or equipment there are three things you must ask yourself:

1. Do I have the expertise and confidence to try this trip?
2. Can I cope mentally and physically?
3. Am I sure that I'm not being too ambitious on my first attempt?

If your answer to these three questions is yes, and you feel that you are capable of such a venture, then this is the book for you. But first, think about your friend. Can you answer 'yes' to all three questions for him or her. And can your friend answer 'yes' too? You must be able to rely upon your companion. If all the answers come up 'yes', then read on.

Use your common sense

Being over-ambitious is a common fault with most first time adventurers. TV and films tend to make everything look easy, with everyone at the end of the film safe and well. But things do go wrong even for the professionals and minor incidents can quickly turn into a major disaster.

In your initial planning you should try to cater

for just such events. That is why you sit down and plan everything first. Common sense tells you it is better to sort problems out on paper rather than on site. After all that is what your planning and preparation are for.

Who does what?

Let's think again about that day-long expedition you and your friend are planning.

Rambling and hiking are pretty similar activities, but there is a difference in the way the groups are made up. Ramblers tend to be in large organized groups or clubs, whilst hikers very often prefer to travel in twos or threes, sometimes in a family group. Many rambling clubs have dozens of members and can be seen in parties of thirty or more walking the hills and dales, but, whatever the party, they always plan their walks with military precision, working out the number of people taking part, the transport needed to get them to their destination and back, a detailed route, what to take in the way of equipment, clothing, safety aids, and finally, the cost. The planning is often carried out by a group of experienced walkers who sit down and draw up individual lists and then compare them to ensure that they have covered everything. This is just what we are going to do.

Ask the experts

The first thing you must both do is to get your parents' permission. Once they agree then you

can sit down and draw up a list of what you want to do, when, where, and how, and what equipment you'll need. Make *separate* lists, and then compare them.

For instance, the date you choose may not be suitable for you both. It might clash with something that your parents want to do with you. So set a date, check it out with everyone and stick to it.

Once you have completed your lists, ask your parents to make one up – then you can see how yours compare with theirs. Remember, adults often have a great deal more experience in these things than you do, so do not be afraid to ask their advice. Try asking the local Scout/Guide or Youth Club leader for help with your plans. You could even ask your teacher. Many schools now take part in lots of outdoor adventures and have some very experienced instructors. Your local library should have useful information in books, leaflets and even maps, and the librarians can often help you to locate addresses of organizations like tourist boards or local rambling clubs.

Let's make our *equipment* list for now. In the next chapter we will think about the best types of clothing to buy; and in Chapter 3 we will discuss map and compass reading, and planning a detailed route.

'Think list'

Right! Now check your equipment list with mine and see how they compare. Remember your list should have been finalized only after you, your friend and your parents got together to discuss each detail.

EQUIPMENT LIST

To carry

lightweight rucksack containing:
map of route
route card (your own detailed plan of your route -
see page 55)
Silva compass
torch with spare batteries
whistle
small plastic pad containing notepad and pencil
first aid pack
money
thermos flask containing hot drink
sandwich/snack box containing food
spare sweater
matchbox survival kit (see page 28)
survival bag or blanket (see page 32)

To wear

strong walking boots/shoes
long woollen socks
waterproof jacket, preferably in bright fluorescent
colour and with thin, separate lining
walking cord trousers* or other suitable trousers
(not man-made fibres)
waterproof trousers*
gaiters*
warm woollen hat
gloves
watch

NOTE: If your waterproof jacket is not a bright colour
buy fluorescent armbands, and fluorescent strips
to fasten to your rucksack. It is important to be seen
by motorists or, in an emergency by rescuers.

* optional

Are our lists the same? Let's go through mine.

As you would expect, the right kind of footwear is very important so a good pair of walking boots or shoes is essential. (More about clothing in the next chapter.) You will also need some specialist items such as a map and a compass (I recommend a Silva compass as this is very light and simple to use – more about this later too). You'll need a torch, whistle, thermos flask for your drinks, a sandwich box, a spare sweater, a waterproof jacket, a notepad and pencil, matchbox survival kit (see page 28) and small first aid pack. Just in case you end up with a blister or two, remember to include plenty of plasters and some antiseptic cream. All of these can be carried on your back quite comfortably in a lightweight rucksack. Some of the items of clothing on my list are marked 'optional'. You would certainly need them for a long expedition, but for a shortish day trip you can manage without if you are sensible.

Finally you may need some money just in case you want to stop off at a café or you need to catch the bus/train home in a hurry. Many ramblers plan stops into their routes so that they can rest and buy the odd present, and as this is your first solo walk it is a good idea if you do the same. It is also a *safety factor*. If you get lost or are late back, at least there is another adult who has seen you en route. Your parents can ring the café or shop to check that you did call in there as planned, and, if something has gone wrong, they will be able to pinpoint *where* it happened more easily. Remember, even the best-planned expeditions can run into a hitch, and you might need to be rescued – you and your sprained ankle.

2

Buying the right clothes

Your first trip may only be for a day or an afternoon, but that is still a long time to be out in the open, so you will need to carry and wear equipment to ensure your safety and comfort. We listed everything you are likely to need on page 13. Now let's discuss the main items of clothing in more detail.

What to wear

Let's start with *socks*. Why? Because it is very important to wear the right type, and you need to buy them before you get your boots, so that you can wear the right socks as you are trying boots on in the shop.

Woollen socks are best, ideally ones that pull up just below the knees. Nylon socks are not recommended as they tend to make your feet sweaty and hot, and encourage blisters.

Now to *boots or shoes*. It is not advisable to walk in trainers or soft-soled shoes as they can cause severe blisters, especially when you have to travel over rough terrain. Walking boots give you the vital grip and support you need to ensure comfort and safety. Unfortunately a good pair of

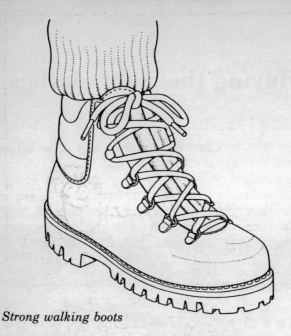

Strong walking boots

boots can be expensive but if you can afford them
I strongly recommend that you do so.

Ex-Army boots will suffice at a pinch (after all,
they were designed for marching long distances –
and I should know being an ex-soldier). But a
word of warning here: if you decide on ex-army
boots, make sure that they have been well and
truly worn in by you first. This goes for all boots,
of course. Never go off on a day's hike in new
boots. Break them in over a couple of weeks by
wearing them for short periods each day.

When you go to buy your boots, take along the
socks you will want to wear on the day, and
remember you are still growing, so do not buy

boots that in a couple of months will be too small
for you.

Never be rushed into buying anything that you
feel is not right. It would be a good idea to take
your mum or dad along with you as they can help
you decide. Do not let the shop owner persuade
you to buy if you are not happy.

The same applies when choosing any of your
clothing – your *waterproof jacket* for instance.
This needs to be large enough to be worn over a
thick sweater and it must be a fluorescent colour
easily spotted by a motorist or (in case you get
lost) rescue teams.

There is a bewilderingly large selection of
waterproof jackets currently on sale in the shops.
Unfortunately many are made from cheap
materials and are not at all suitable for any outdoor activity.

There is a vast difference in both price and
quality, and, as always, it is a case of choosing the
right one for the job. At the cheaper end of the
market you can buy lightweight, windproof
jackets for just a few pounds, but remember they
are windproof and not waterproof. When wet the
cheaper garments can be hopeless, as they do not
provide you with the protection you will need in
a heavy downpour, and in most cases they are
designed for style rather than comfort and safety.

Never be scared to try on your waterproofs in
the shop. Ask questions and test the quality. For
instance, pull lightly on the sleeves to see if the
stitching comes apart at the shoulder. (You do not
have to rip the jacket apart, just a gentle tug!) Try
the hood if the jacket has one. Why? Well, many
of the cheaper jackets have very small hoods and

Waterproof jacket. Note the close-fitting hood, which protects the bottom of the face

would not be suitable for your use. A hood must, of course, give protection to the back and top of the head, but it should also be able to draw together, to protect the ears and cheeks. Contrary to what you may read in some books, it is safer to have a hood that fastens across the face (covering

the mouth and cheeks) with Velcro rather than a
string or cord fastener. Many unsuspecting hikers
have been blown off their feet and nearly died of
strangulation because they were unable to loosen
the tie cords on their hoods.

What to look for in choosing your waterproof jacket

1. Hood large enough to cover the head, cheeks
    and chin
2. Velcro neck fastener
3. Large collar
4. Zip and Velcro fastener
5. Large, deep, flap-covered pockets with Velcro
    fastening for quick easy access.
6. Long sleeves with fluorescent strips, Velcro
    fastener or elasticated cuff
7. Long jacket body, preferably just below the
    knees
8. Bright international recognition colours: red,
    orange or yellow.

The waterproof test

A useful tip to test the waterproofing on material
is to hold it close to your mouth and breathe
heavily on it, especially where there is a seam.

If the material is cheap it will immediately
allow the moisture from your breath to seep

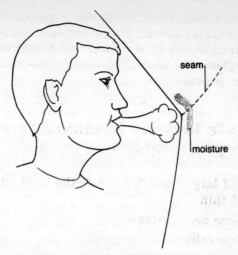

Testing a seam for waterproofing

through. If this happens it is a good indication that the material is not waterproof and would in fact allow water in, or that the seams are not properly waterproofed.

By the same token, if the material does not allow water in, it will also prevent condensation from getting out.

Ideally what you want is a jacket that is waterproof on the outside, with a thin, separate inner lining to prevent condensation building up. Such jackets are available, but they can be costly.

Think before you buy

Once you have gained confidence and begun to venture a little further afield – perhaps walking across mountains or moorlands – you will quickly appreciate just how vital to your safety your waterproofs are. Do not be tempted to buy cheap. Remember, the higher you climb, the colder and wetter it gets.

Unfortunately accidents do happen in every walk of life, but many can easily be avoided especially if you are wearing the right protective clothing. Out in open country the COLD . . . WET . . . WIND . . . are the three main potential killers, and every year people die (especially inexperienced hikers) not because they fell off a cliff or were trapped down a flooded mine, but because they underestimated the way the cold, wet and wind can seep away your body energy and heat. When this happens you quickly become another HYPOTHERMIA statistic, and we all know that hypothermia kills.

Hypothermia comes about as a result of loss of body heat, caused by excessive cold or exposure to wet and wind. The body temperature is lowered to a level where death occurs. So you see how important it is to choose the right equipment and clothing for your safety.

DO NOT BUY CHEAP. It is better to spend a few extra pounds and get something that will give you the protection you need than to spend foolishly and buy rubbish. When I was an instructor in the army I remember one old general telling me that the only way to buy cheaply was to buy expensive. 'Buy something good now, and it will last you a long time. Buy something cheap and you will have to buy again very soon,' he said. Think about it.

Safety and comfort

The same rules apply to *waterproof trousers*. Make sure that they are long enough to cover the whole legs and top of the feet. I personally like the waist to be elasticated. This allows me to slip them on and off easily.

I also prefer waterproof trousers with bottoms wide enough for me to slip over my boots. Some have a small zip at the bottom of the legs to allow for this.

When walking in wet weather, it is best to have all the weight on your shoulders and not on your legs or in your pockets. So it is necessary to choose waterproof trousers that will not be too heavy and cumbersome. The lighter your clothing and equipment is the less weight you have to lug around. However, do not sacrifice safety for comfort. A great deal of your precious body heat is lost from around the thighs and legs and a good pair of

Waterproof trousers

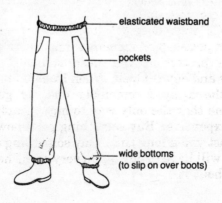

elasticated waistband

pockets

wide bottoms
(to slip on over boots)

waterproof trousers is just as important as the jacket especially when you are walking in adverse weather. It is wise to buy waterproof trousers with pockets in them, as it can be very uncomfortable reaching into your inner trouser pockets each time you want to get to your handkerchief or purse.

Many hikers wear strong cord trousers and prefer gaiters to waterproofs but walking cords can be very expensive to buy. Gaiters are fine when walking in long grass or over rough bracken and heather, but along dusty tracks and roads can make the legs hot.

Because the first hike you are planning is local and not over rough, high terrain there is no point at this stage in investing in expensive walking trousers, though obviously if you can afford them then buy some, but, as with the boots, socks and jacket, remember that you are still growing. For local walks, jeans can be used as a substitute

Walking cords and gaiters

but only as a last resort. When wet they tend to
chafe the inside of the thighs and also take a long
time to dry. The most essential requirement is
that your trousers should be natural fibre (such as
cotton), not man-made.

3

Survival equipment

As an aid to your safety, why not make yourself
up a small survival kit to take along with you?

Why a survival kit? Well, apart from giving you
a few extra safety items to call upon in an
emergency, having a survival kit with you is a
great morale booster and providing you do not
make it too large and cumbersome there should
be no trouble carrying it around with you. In fact
you can make one that will fit into a matchbox
quite easily.

The most important thing to remember when
putting together any survival kit is that every
item must have at least two uses, if not more. For
instance, a piece of chalk can obviously be used

for marking a trail or leaving a message, but it can also be used to help settle an upset tummy. Soldiers sometimes used crushed chalk to stop cuts and scratches from bleeding and large amounts of crushed chalk can be used as an improvised water filter. So you see how important it is where possible to include items that have a multiple use.

Making a matchbox survival kit

Ask Mum or Dad to give you a new box of matches (the smaller size, which will fit easily into your pocket, not the large family size). Empty the matches out on a sheet of newspaper on the table. Take the inner tray of the matchbox (the section that holds the matches) and place it on a plate, then take a lit candle and carefully melt some of the candle wax into the bottom of the matchbox to a depth of about 2 millimetres.

Whilst the wax is soft gently place some of the matches in and cover them with another thin layer of wax, at the same time drop in three or four different sized fish hooks, a needle, safety pin and half a dozen straight pins.

The wax will harden around the matches keeping them waterproof and will hold the fish hooks, pins, etc., firmly.

Take a short stub of a pencil and wrap a sheet of notepaper around it, then wind about 10 metres of fishing line and sewing cotton around the paper and put it into a balloon. To secure the balloon slip on a couple of elastic bands.

Take a safety razor blade or surgical scalpel and

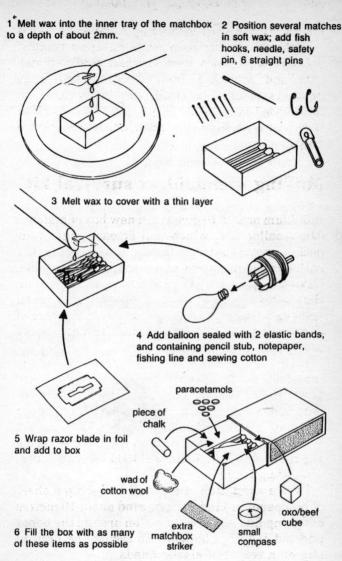

1 Melt wax into the inner tray of the matchbox to a depth of about 2mm.

2 Position several matches in soft wax; add fish hooks, needle, safety pin, 6 straight pins

3 Melt wax to cover with a thin layer

4 Add balloon sealed with 2 elastic bands, and containing pencil stub, notepaper, fishing line and sewing cotton

5 Wrap razor blade in foil and add to box

6 Fill the box with as many of these items as possible

paracetamols

piece of chalk

wad of cotton wool

extra matchbox striker

small compass

oxo/beef cube

Matchbox survival kit

wrap it in a 15cm square of cooking foil. Place inside the matchbox.

The following should also fit into your matchbox kit if you have packed everything properly:

A few paracetamol tablets
Oxo or beef cube
A small compass
An extra matchbox striker
A small wad of cotton wool
A piece of chalk.

You can, of course, make your own survival pack up and it does not have to be in a matchbox either. If you wish you could make one up in an old cigarette packet, spare fountain pen case, or just a small plastic bag. Whatever you use, remember it is a survival pack and only to be used in an emergency so do not over pack – and everthing that is packed must have a multiple use.

Take a simple match: after having been used to light your fire the wasted stalk can be used as a

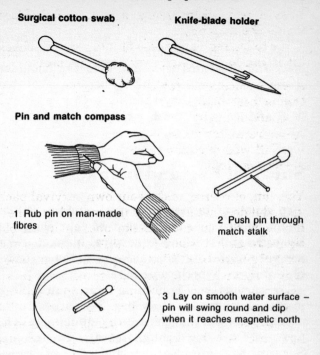

Surgical cotton swab

Knife-blade holder

Pin and match compass

1 Rub pin on man-made fibres

2 Push pin through match stalk

3 Lay on smooth water surface – pin will swing round and dip when it reaches magnetic north

Uses of a match

surgical cotton swab, a crude paintbrush, a surgical knife-blade holder, even a compass holder. Take one of your pins or needles from the pack, and rub it against some man-made fibres. (It will then become magnetized having picked up the static electricity from your clothing.) Push it through the match stalk and lay it gently on a smooth water surface away from any iron or metal. As it settles on the water it will dip when it begins to point to the magnetic north.

Soldiers make two, sometimes three, basic survival kits. One is hidden within their uniform, another is made up and fastened to their webbing belt, and the third is strapped to the shoulder straps of their rucksack. If they become separated from all of these they then have to live off the land and use what mother nature can provide.

Survival bag and blanket

Two excellent items of survival equipment you might like to consider as part of your shopping list are a survival bag or survival blanket. Both are very useful items to have in an emergency, especially in hypothermia cases.

The survival bag is nothing more than a large plastic sheet made into a bag. Its purpose is to protect you from the elements by climbing into it, and some are big enough to take two people. Survival bags are ideal for wind and wet protection but do not ward off the cold. However, if insulated from the ground and then covered with a coat or blanket they do help the body inside to retain heat.

The survival blanket is just that, a blanket, but a blanket made from very strong tin foil. Its purpose is to reflect your body heat back and it is wrapped around you as a blanket would be. At a push it can be used as an improvised shelter (as can the survival bag), to carry items of clothing in, and even as a marker panel.

Both are light to carry and a must for anyone who intends to do a lot of hill walking. I personally recommend that you take at least one of them with you on your hike.

Dress for safety

Even on a short hike, think safety at all times. Check your equipment thoroughly before you go. Make sure you take everything on your list, but don't weigh yourself down with useless extras. Put your matchbox survival kit in your pocket, not in your rucksack. Tie your compass and whistle around your neck so they won't get lost. Dress for safety and you'll be able to meet any challenge.

4

Maps, compasses and planning your route

An afternoon out in your local park or the nearest open space will give you the opportunity to test out your new equipment and in particular your map and compass reading. Map reading is not nearly as difficult as some people make out. Once you can read a map properly a whole new world opens before you every time you travel outdoors.

Map-reading made easy

To become confident with your map-reading it is important that you treat the map as an open book. Remember a map is nothing more than a series of lines, dots and symbols used to make a picture of the ground spread out before you. Once you have learnt to recognize these, map-reading becomes easy.

Each symbol, line or dot tells a story. They help the map makers to produce accurate information (taken mostly from aerial photographs) that is easily understandable to a map reader. Across the whole of the map you will see a series of horizontal and vertical lines, called *grid lines*, which divide the map into square sections. And running

up the side and across the bottom of the map is a series of numbers, with the lowest figure in the bottom left hand corner. Using these grid lines and numbers a map reader is able to find a location accurately to within a few metres.

At the bottom or side of your map you will find the *scale line*. Your map is, of course, much smaller than the land it shows, and the scale line enables you to calculate the real distance between two points. Look at this illustration. The scale line shows you that the *real* distance from one grid square to the next is 1km. If you measure the distance *on the map* you will find it is 2cm. So the scale of this map is 1km : 2cm (2cm on the map is equal to 1km on the ground).

To find out how far the distance is between two points, you simply measure the distance between them on the map (let's say it is 3cm) and then read this figure off against your scale line (so we find that 3cm=1.5km). It is as easy as that.

A really excellent book, which gives lots of clear helpful information on map reading is *Follow the map* by John G. Wilson, published by A & C Black. It is well worth buying a copy, or borrowing it from your library. Your library will probably have other books too. Ask your parents to help you as you practise your map reading. Better still, get some advice from your Scout or Guide leaders. All Scout and Guide leaders have to be proficient map readers, so they can give you excellent advice. Another source of information is the video or cassette training tapes which are widely available.

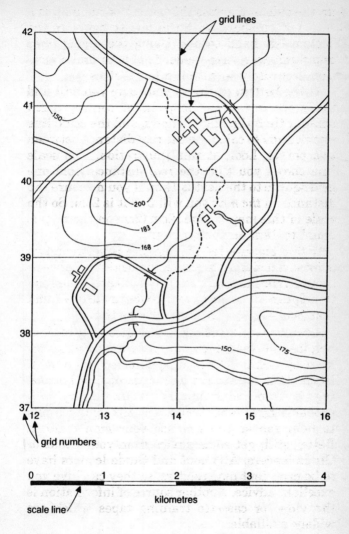

Section of map showing grid lines, grid numbers and scale line

Finding a grid reference

Here is a simple example of basic map-reading that we can do together. Let's say we want to draw up a route, giving the correct grid references. This illustration shows a small section

Finding a grid reference

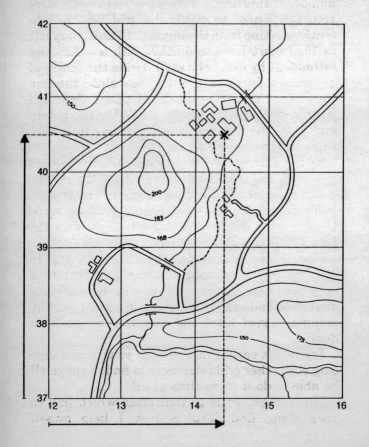

of our map, with grid lines and numbers. We have
decided we want to make for the point that I have
marked with a cross on the map. It is this spot
that we want to find a grid reference for.

Right, here we go. To find the grid reference of
my chosen point, I first run my finger along the
numbers at the bottom of the map until I come to
the line just to the left of my cross. I read off the
number of this line, which is 14. To be even more
accurate, I need to divide the grid line up into
tenths starting from the number 14 and going left
to 15. I don't have to do this with a ruler, just
estimate it by eye. Let's say I decide the centre of
my cross is four tenths of the way along the line
from 14 to 15. I've now got the first part of my grid
reference: 14 (for the line to the left of the point),
and 4 (for the number of tenths along from that
line), to give me the figure 144.

Next I run my finger *up* the left-hand edge of
the map, and this time I read off the figure just
below my cross (40). I now estimate the tenths,
and decide that my cross is exactly halfway up to
the next grid line: five tenths, which gives me the
figure 5. So my figure is 405.

I put these two figures together: 144 405 to
give me my *grid reference number*. This is a
very accurate figure, and it will be easy for
anyone to find exactly where we are going, just by
using the grid lines and numbers as we have
done.

Try it. It's easy! Practise with your friend, setting each other grid references to find. Soon you'll
be able to do it in no time at all.

The hardest bit is to remember which line to
read along first. This is how I help myself

remember. I say to myself 'FIRST I MUST WALK
DOWN THE PASSAGE BEFORE I CAN CLIMB
THE LADDER.'

Learning your symbols

On your map all signs, lines and dots are called
symbols or *conventional signs*. The map makers
put them there to help you identify places more
easily. For instance, roads that have a proper tar-
macadam surface are marked with both a letter
and a number.

Main roads will have the letter A and a number,
for example, A59. Secondary roads will display
the letter B and a number, for example B56. Main
(A) roads may be labelled A59(T) – the (T) stands
for 'trunk', which means they are major routes.

Motorways are clearly marked with a capital M
and a number, the M1 for instance. Motorways
are generally shown as thick lines, while main

and secondary roads are shown as thinner lines, usually in a different colour.

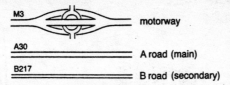

Tracks, trails and footpaths are easily identifiable as shown.

Rivers are shown as thin blue lines with the name of the river printed above.

At the bottom or at the side of your map you will see a section (the *key*) that helps you to identify the various symbols and shows the colours used to distinguish the different types of roads. Use this key to find the meaning of all the symbols.

Contour lines

Another important map-reading skill is the ability to interpret the contour lines. These are the thin irregular black, brown or orange lines spread right across the map. Some, you will notice, have numbers written on them at inter-

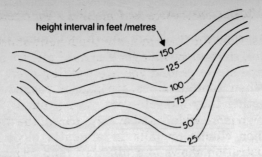

height interval in feet /metres

150
125
100
75
50
25

The numbers give the height above sea level. Modern maps show the height in metres, but older maps may show feet. Look at the key to find out which.

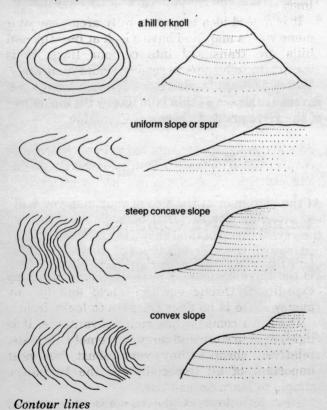

a hill or knoll

uniform slope or spur

steep concave slope

convex slope

Contour lines

vals. Contour lines indicate the height above sea level, so that you can get a mental picture of the shape of the ground you are walking over.

When contour lines are shown packed close together they indicate very steep ground. When shown more widely and evenly spaced, the ground either climbs or falls in a gentle slope. The illustration shows four different land formations and how they would appear on a map, as contour lines.

It is a good idea to go to a hilly area near your home with a map, and have a look at how the real hills are translated into contour lines. It is important to be able to read contours accurately. You don't want to plan a walk which brings you to the bottom of a steep hill right at the end, when you are ready to drop from exhaustion.

So you can see that it isn't too difficult to learn to read a map. What you have to do now is go outside and practise.

Using a Silva compass

I mentioned earlier that my personal preference is the Silva compass. I have used one on all my expeditions throughout the world and for my money there is no finer compass to learn from.

The Silva compass has many advantages. It is light, easy to store and carry, extremely accurate, relatively cheap to buy, very robust, but most important of all (especially for the beginner), simple to learn on and use.

First let's look at the compass closely, and

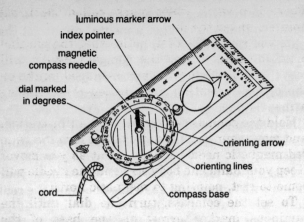

luminous marker arrow
index pointer
magnetic
compass needle
dial marked
in degrees
orienting arrow
orienting lines
cord
compass base

Silva compass

discover how it works. The illustration will help
you to identify all the different parts as we
discuss them.

Hold the compass so that the cord is nearest to
your body. You will see a luminous marker arrow
on the rectangular-shaped compass base, and the
magnetic compass needle in its liquid-filled
circular container which is surrounded by a dial.

The red end of the needle will always point to
magnetic north (more about magnetic north later
in the chapter) unless there is something made of
iron or steel — a car, bicycle or iron gate, for
instance — nearby, when it will be thrown off
course.

Look at the dial now, and you will see that it is
marked with four letters N (north), S (south), E
(east) and W (west) and with numbers, from 0 to
360. These numbers are called *degrees*. You can
rotate the dial to move the degree markings.

There is a small white mark, called the index pointer, under the dial.

As you rotate the dial, notice that the parallel orienting lines under the compass needle will move with it. Notice the arrow-shaped marks on the central orienting lines, called the orienting arrow.

Hold the compass as shown in the illustration, and move your body in a circle. See how the little red magnetic needle swings about as you move? Keep your hand and body still and the needle will come to rest, pointing to magnetic north.

To set the compass, turn the dial until the luminous marker arrow on the base of the compass, the index pointer and the letter N on the dial are lined up. Now, holding the compass steady, turn your body until the red magnetic needle is lined up on the N. The compass is now set to magnetic north, and you are ready to orientate your map and yourself.

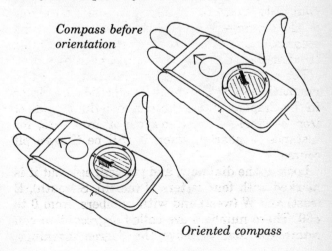

Compass before orientation

Oriented compass

Orientation

Place the compass gently on a flat piece of ground, keeping the needle lined up with the letter N and the luminous marker arrow. Take out your map and open it. Lay it alongside the compass with the top of the map pointing in the same direction as the needle. You can now place the compass on top of the map, making sure the magnetic needle is still aligned on the letter N and marker arrow.

If you stand at the bottom of your map, looking along the compass arrow and needle, then the map, the compass and you are all aligned on magnetic north!

Oriented map and compass

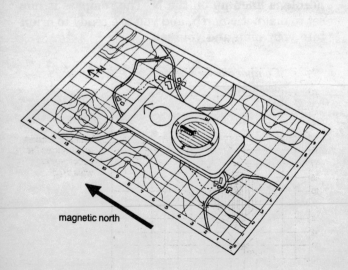

magnetic north

Taking a bearing

You have learned to read a map, and how to set your compass and align your map with it. The next stage is to use your compass to take a bearing.

What is a bearing? Well, it's a measurement of the *direction* of your route, measured as an angle from north. For example, if you wanted to go due east, your bearing would be 90 degrees from north (look at the figures on your compass dial).

Got the idea? With a Silva compass you can use your luminous marker arrow to check your bearing very easily. Here's how.

Place the compass on your map so that the outside edge of the base links the point on the map

Taking a bearing

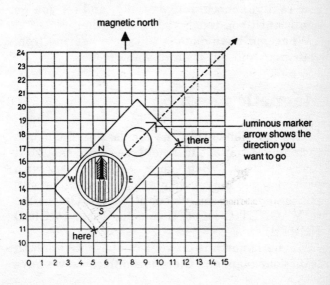

where you are standing (HERE) and the point you want to get to (THERE). The luminous marker arrow must be pointing in the same direction as THERE. The illustration (page 47) shows you how.

Now turn the dial on the compass until the letter N on the dial points to the top of the map (north) and the orienting lines inside the container are parallel with the vertical grid lines on the map. The little orienting arrow inside the container should be pointing to the top of the map.

Lift the compass off the map and turn your body until the red end of the magnetic needle is directly over the arrow inside the dial.

The direction you want to go is now along the line of the luminous marker arrow at the top of the compass.

Line the luminous marker up with a landmark and off you go. When you reach your landmark, just realign, check your bearing, and off you go again until you reach your destination.

What you have done is to take a bearing from your map and put it on to your compass.

Magnetic north

I have mentioned that the compass needle points to 'magnetic north'. It is not true north, though it is pretty close. When you set your compass with your map you may have noticed two small arrows in the margin of the map or at the top. One points to MAGNETIC NORTH and the other to GRID NORTH.

Magnetic north is on your compass. Grid north is on your map, and there is a difference we have

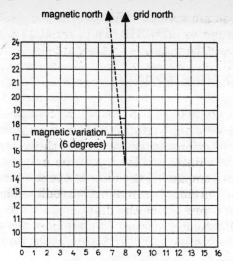

Magnetic north and grid north

to allow for if we are to be completely accurate.
This is how we do it:

Between the two arrows on the top of the map
you will see some figures, the *magnetic variation*
between grid north and magnetic north. (This is
approximately 7 degrees in the British Isles.)

From grid to mag

After plotting a bearing on your map and setting
your compass to it you must remember to ADD the
variation. For example, the bearing from HERE to
THERE on the map may read 40 degrees. When
you have set your compass along this line you *add*

the variation shown; let's say it is 7 degrees. So your compass dial will in fact be set at 47 degrees.

From mag to grid

When you take a bearing on a distant object, holding the compass in your hand, place your compass down on the map at the point HERE. Line the magnetic needle and the orienting lines up with the grid lines pointing to the top of the map.

Both the map and the compass are now set. All you have to do to convert the magnetic bearing (the one on your compass) to a grid bearing (the one on your map) is to SUBTRACT the variation. In this case the 7 degrees.

Allowing for the magnetic variation

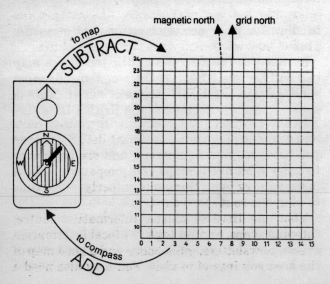

REMEMBER, to CONVERT a bearing

FROM GRID TO MAG . . . (map to compass)
. . . ADD

FROM MAG TO GRID . . . (compass to map)
. . . SUBTRACT

Practise pacing

Before you go on your trip, get out and practise your map-reading in the nearby park or woods. See how many of the symbols you can recognize on the ground from those shown on the map.

Practise taking bearings from the compass and following them, and at the same time learn to pace yourself.

Remember you are not soldiers, and you are not on a route march either. Hiking is meant to be enjoyable. A few introductory walks will get you fit, break in your walking boots, and allow you to perfect your map-reading and compass skills.

Planning your route

Remember when you sat down with your parents and friend to plan your equipment list? Since then you have got your equipment, and are beginning to know a bit about maps and compasses. Now it is time to try everything out properly – it's time to plan the route for your trip.

Visit the library, tourist information centre, camping shops, and get together local information sheets, newsletters, guidebooks and a good map of the area you intend to visit. You may also need a bus or train timetable. Spread all this material out on a table alongside your map. You will need some paper and pencils, for making notes and plotting your route.

Do not be too ambitious. It being your first hiking trip you will be practising map-reading skills and probably wearing new boots and clothing.

Think carefully about *how far* you are planning to travel. For your first attempt, you should plan to walk not more than 8–10 miles (12–16 kilometres), and I suggest that you allow 5–6 hours to complete your journey. This allows plenty of time for rest and meal breaks, and for taking a look at the countryside around you. If you find you're still raring to go at the end of this trip, you can always plan something longer next time.

When? What? Where? How much?

Firstly decide *when* you would like to go – perhaps during school holidays or at a weekend.

On most weekends there are lots of other hikers around and this is a safety bonus for you. You could go on a weekday, but take into consideration that there are lots of heavy vehicles moving around on the roads and they can be dangerous to hikers. Once you have fixed a date stick to it.

Now decide on *what* you want to do. Is it to be a country lane walk or perhaps a trek across open countryside? As it is your first solo walk I would advise a local country lane and track route, one that will not be too demanding physically.

Next question is '*Where?*' Choose somewhere

easy to reach from your home. Ideally you should be able to set off walking practically from your back door or the local park. Think about how you are going to get back too. Is the walk going to be circular – so that you come back to your starting point – or are you going to rely on public transport to get you home?

Which brings us to the last question, 'How much?' This is one of the most important questions of all. How much is your adventure going to cost? Calculate everything carefully: food, equipment, fares, and make sure you add an extra sum for emergency expenses – extra fares in case you get stranded, telephone calls, a meal in a café if you miss a bus and are starving.

Your detailed plan

Study your information sheet and maps carefully and if everyone is in agreement, draw up your intended route on a sheet of paper. Double check that you have calculated the distance accurately, and that it is not too long for you to manage in the time available. Decide on several stopping places. Note the bus routes, and make a list of prominent landmarks that may be useful to help you check your map-reading, and as pace-markers.

Stopping places are important for two reasons. Firstly they ensure you do take a rest – remember, this is your first real long hike. They also help keep you safe. Using your map, follow the contours of the route and try to ensure that your stops are easily found: the village post office, for instance, or a small farm by a bridge. The more contact you have with people who see you when you are out walking the safer it is. Especially if the two of you are girls.

Discuss your route with your parents before you make your detailed route card. Make a copy of your route card (or photocopy it) and leave it with them. It is important that they know exactly what route you are taking so that they can contact you in an emergency, or work out where you are if you get lost or delayed.

Finally, two very important factors: the weather and the light. It is quite dark by 4.30 p.m. in mid winter so you should aim to be safely at home by then if you are planning a winter hike. The weather is more difficult to predict. A good tip is, close to the day you intend to walk, check the weather forecast. It may be that you will have to take an extra sweater or waterproof, or even postpone your walk.

Better safe than sorry. There is always another day.

ROUTE CARD

Sunday 15th July HIKE OVER YORKSHIRE MOORS

Distance Ten (10) miles (16 km) ....

Weather conditions ....

ETD (Estimated time of departure) 0900 hrs ....

ETR (Estimated time of return) 1600 hrs ....

Numbers in party (two) EDDIE McGEE , VERA McGEE ....

ROUTE

Stage 1 .... Depart from Pateley Bridge car park
heading west along the B6265 to road junction
at Greenhow Hill village (approximately 2 miles -
3.2 km). Map grid reference 114 642 . ETA (estimated
time of arrival) 1000 hrs . Greenhow village post
office ..... <u>First stop</u>.

Stage 2 .... Turn north across moors on magnetic
bearing of 25 degrees for approximately 3 miles
(4.8 km) stopping at map grid reference 110 705
Raygill House. ETA 1200 hrs .....<u>Second stop</u>.

Stage 3 .... Turn due east down farm track across
river bridge to Bouthwaite, grid reference 125 712 .
Turn south along the northern side of Gouthwaite
Reservoir to village of Wath, grid reference 147 678,
approximately 3 miles (4.8 km). ETA 1400 hrs ......
<u>Third stop</u>.

Stage 4 .... Continue due south to Pateley Bridge village
car park. Grid reference 159 655 approximately 2 miles
(3.2 km). ETA 1530/1600 hrs .... <u>Final stop.</u>

ESCAPE ROUTE IN EMERGENCY
Head for lower ground, swinging right off main route .

Route card for walk in Yorkshire Moors

Think safety

As with all outdoor adventure activities you must allow for a sudden change in the weather and therefore you plan into your route an EMERGENCY escape.

If you look at my route you will notice that it does in fact go around in a (very rough!) circle as will most of your hikes. To ensure that I did not become bored whilst walking, I planned the route to include road, track and moorland, but most important of all, I allowed myself sufficient time to reach my stop points. In an emergency all I had to do was to get down to the nearest road and walk safely back. You should plan your walks so that the road is always in view or very close.

The map on this page shows my route. You can find a more detailed map of the area on Ordnance Survey Landranger (1:50 000) map number 99. Safety factors were always in mind when I planned my route: I started by climbing up the steep ground first whilst I was still fresh, then walked across the high moorlands early in the morning. This way I took advantage of any good weather, and used the best light of the day to enjoy the view.

So you see there are many safety factors to consider, even when planning a simple weekend hike. The more planning and preparation you do, the safer and more enjoyable your hike will be. Once out in the open away from those familiar landmarks you really begin to appreciate just how important your ability to map-read is and if it is a cold, wet, windy day, you will be glad you packed your waterproofs, a hot drink, and sandwiches.

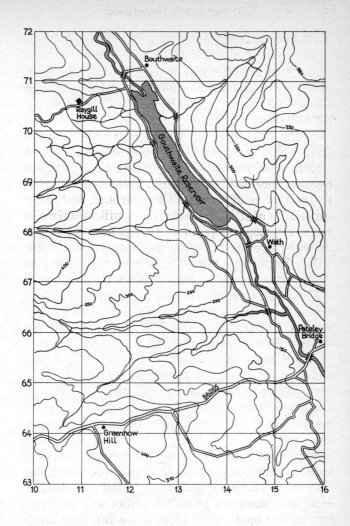

Hike over Yorkshire Moors: map of area covered

Whilst in open country you will have a good opportunity to practise your map-reading, especially if you allow time to keep stopping for a few minutes between stages to get your bearings.

The more you use your map and compass the safer you will be. If you are going up to high ground, note where any mountain rescue centres are situated. You might just need their help, so take this sensible precaution.

It is your first unchaperoned adventure, so it is important that all goes well. Remember your parents are trusting you to ensure that it does, and that you will come to no harm. If you have any doubts at all, check them out with your parents . . . NOW.

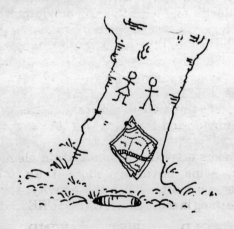

5

Staying safe outdoors . . . the weather

You've planned your route. You are properly
equipped and properly prepared, so you should be
quite safe. But there is no point in going out in
the countryside without thinking about what to
do in an emergency. So the next three chapters
will be about survival in the worst sorts of
emergencies: getting lost in unfamiliar open
country in adverse weather conditions, coping
with injuries and with the loss of equipment.

Let's hope it never happens to you, but if you've
faced the possibility that it *might* happen, you
know what the risks are and can think out
exactly what you would do to stay safe. Then
you'll be able to cope.

First, let's think about natural hazards: driving
rain, thunder and lightning, fog and snow.

All outdoors activities have a certain element of
danger, some obviously more than others.
However, no matter what the activity, they all
have one thing in common . . . . EXPOSURE . . . . to the

COLD . . . . WET . . . . WIND

We mentioned hypothermia in Chapter 2.
People who become hypothermia cases do so
without realizing it, especially if they do not have

the right protective clothing and equipment to ward it off. Hypothermia tends to creep up on you very slowly and, when you least expect it, it strikes suddenly.

REMEMBER . . . hypothermia is non-selective and will attack people of any age group, young or old, so be prepared. Hypothermia can kill.

Protect yourself against the elements by wearing the right clothing and carrying the right equipment). Avoid hypothermia by taking simple precautions. In other words do not put yourself in danger. Consider possible hypothermia situations in your route planning, and aim to avoid them altogether.

One way to ensure that you do not get caught out in the open unprotected is to try and plan your route away from high ground, moorlands and marshes where it is almost certain you will end up getting wet. If you have to travel through these areas keep a sharp lookout for any weather change, and for any unusual physical and mental signs your friend may be showing.

Lagging behind . . . slowing down . . . slurring of speech . . . irrational behaviour . . . excessive sweating . . . skin becoming very pallid . . . sinking into a deep depression and becoming very sulky . . . these are all hypothermia symptoms. Learn to recognize these changes in behaviour not only in your friend but in yourself.

Do not push yourselves too hard. Stay within your physical limits and make sure you have at least one good meal a day, preferably two: a good breakfast and evening meal. Use your rest areas

sensibly and whilst resting protect yourself from the chilling wind and driving rain. If you feel the weather worsening get off the high ground down to safety.

There is always another day. BETTER TO BE SAFE THAN SORRY.

Head for shelter

If you are unfortunate enough to get caught in a sudden weather change and you are forced to stop, seek shelter out of the wind. Put on your waterproofs and check out your escape route.

DO NOT ATTEMPT TO BLUNDER ON. Stay in your shelter unless you know for certain that you can safely reach your destination.

If you have to seek shelter off your route remember to get back on the same course (compass bearing) when the weather lifts. If possible shelter in a building or nearby farmhouse. If there is a telephone nearby head for it and let Mum and Dad know how and where you are. All telephone kiosks have individual telephone numbers so remember to tell Mum and Dad the number. Look for telephone kiosks when planning your route; they are clearly marked on most maps. However, do not expect them to be on top of the moors and mountains. Kiosks have to be maintained so it is almost certain that there will be an access road nearby.

Another useful tip is to look at your map and try to spot pylons or telephone wire symbols. Many people have managed to survive and reach safety simply by following them. But I do stress it is important to have a map to check your route, otherwise you could end up walking further into isolated countryside.

Sometimes when the weather becomes really bad, especially during a severe storm, you may not have time to reach a building so you will have to make do with the best shelter to hand. Try sheltering beneath a rock overhang, up against a stone wall, under a stone bridge, or even a tree if there is no lightning around.

The most important thing is to stay together, and keep as dry as possible.

REMEMBER . . . the higher you go the colder it gets. Walking the hills during a thunderstorm can be very frightening and extremely dangerous, especially if it is dark, and the ground beneath you is wet and soggy. As I have said before . . . DO NOT BLUNDER ON. Fortunately most storms take time to build up so keep an eye on the

weather. Mother Nature will always help you if you listen to her.

When a storm is approaching, clouds begin to mass and the sky darkens as the light begins to fade. In the distance you will probably hear the dull clap of thunder and maybe even spot a streak of lightning over on the distant horizon. If you do, that is Mother Nature telling you to beware, so heed her warnings.

ALWAYS read up and listen to the weather forecast before setting off. That way you will avoid trouble.

What to do in a thunderstorm

As the storm approaches and the sky gets darker and darker, the wind will increase, the temperature will drop quickly and down will come the rain. All around you thunder will be crashing around the hills and the lightning will streak across the skies. When the storm is directly above you it will seem as if the whole heavens have descended upon you. But do not be afraid, soon it will pass and, providing you are wearing your waterproofs and take sensible precautions, you will be safe.

What about being struck by lightning? Well, no one can give you a firm answer on that question. Lightning is unpredictable and can strike anywhere, even if you feel you are fully protected. Indeed people who thought they were safe inside a building have been struck by lightning whilst others caught outdoors survived without any problems.

Many experts claim that if you are caught out in the open during a thunderstorm you should avoid resting beneath trees or alongside metal gates and fences as these attract lightning. If I am caught in the hills during a storm I personally prefer to sit in the open, preferably on a featureless slope, having removed anything metal that could attract a possible lightning strike.

If you have a tent with you and you are caught in a thunderstorm with no available shelter, put your tent up and rest inside. Providing you leave anything metal some distance outside (your cooking utensils, stove, etc.) you should come to no harm.

Fog

Getting caught in thick fog can be both dangerous and scary but, providing you have your compass and map handy, you should have no problems getting back to safety. The obvious dangers are walking over cliff edges, and falling into streams, or pot holes, but your map will tell you what kind of terrain lies ahead, and if you stay together and do not panic you will be OK. Walking in the fog slows you down so allow for this when working out your estimated arrival time at your destination.

A good tip is to have your whistle and torch handy in case you need to signal to each other. If you have them, wear your luminous arm bands.

Certainly wear your waterproofs as mist and fog can be very damp and cold and will quickly sap your energy. If you are on high, isolated ground and you feel that the mist is going to be persistent you would be wise to get down off the hills as soon as possible

In really dense fog noises become muffled and it can be difficult to distinguish many natural sounds, so if the area you are walking in has lots of streams be sure to use your map and compass and . . .

KEEP YOUR EARS AND EYES OPEN

Snow

Walking in a soft, gentle snowfall can be quite pleasant, especially when you are on home territory and able to recognize known landmarks, but remember that gentle snowfall can quickly turn into a raging blizzard. Winds scream and howl as gusts tug at your clothing and sweep you off your feet. The driving snow makes it impossible to see where you are going and in no time you are completely off course.

Only a fool attempts to walk during snow storms, especially on high ground. Stay safe. If you have to go walking, keep to low land and always stay on well marked tracks and roads.

Next to being caught in a blizzard, a winter white-out is probably the most frightening weather hazard you can encounter. This is when the temperature drops suddenly and in seconds (even though the skies may have been clear a moment ago) the white-out is upon you. One minute you can see for miles, suddenly you are shrouded in swirling, driving snow, where visibility is down to zero. Any chance of continuing is gone. In seconds you can be completely disoriented and hopelessly lost.

What to do in a white-out

Stop immediately and put on your protective clothing, spare sweaters, etc. If possible seek shelter behind a rock or overhang, even a tree or stone wall will do. Take out your map and compass (take care they do not blow away) and pinpoint your present location. Wait a short while to see if the white-out passes quickly; most only last a short time then blow out.

If the storm looks like lasting, try to get into whatever shelter you can, and keep warm and dry. Pages 88–91 tell you more about building a snow shelter.

International distress calls

If by misfortune you do become lost or even separated from your companion(s) you must immediately stop walking and re-check your location. Try not to panic. If visibility and time are on your side, retrace your steps and get back on course.

Check your position by setting the map as described earlier and look for any prominent landmarks easily recognizable both on the ground and the map. A lone mountain or hill can be your first point of reference. If you are lucky you may be able to spot a distant church with a steeple, or a wide bend in a nearby river, and if it is dark you can very often be guided by a glow in the sky from a nearby town. Railway lines also make excellent reference points and will be clearly marked on your map.

Panic and fear will be your worst enemies. Try to control them. If you have become separated from a friend or main party try shouting for help. Better still, use your whistle and use the international rescue calls: six blasts of the whistle (from you at ten second intervals) answered by your rescuers by three blasts from their whistle. If you have a torch, flash it six times every minute or so, and keep a look out for your rescuers' answering flashes. You could try waving a brightly coloured object to attract their attention or you could use something in your rucksack to make a noise with. As a last resort, light a fire, but make sure that it is safe to do so. The last thing you want is to start a moorland fire.

The most important thing is not to give up. By all means sit down and take stock. But do not under any circumstance blunder on. If you do, you could end up in an even worse situation.

Stop, think, look, listen

Now you see why I advised you to start off taking gentle hikes locally until you have gained sufficient experience and confidence to venture further afield.

Even the most experienced adventurers fear being caught in adverse conditions on the hills. COLD . . . WET . . . WIND . . . can kill even in mild conditions up there in the hills. So think before you set out. Remember the old Army phrase:

IF IN DOUBT . . . KEEP OUT.

When danger threatens

STOP . . . THINK . . . LOOK . . . LISTEN

The same rules for survival apply no matter where you decide to venture. Just because you are travelling in a hot climate does not mean that you will be free from environmental dangers. Floods, blizzards, and storms happen in other countries. I have been travelling across the hot desert during the day and in the early hours of the morning been covered in thick frost. Mother Nature can play some funny tricks. So always be on your guard.

6

Staying safe outdoors . . . coping with injuries

In and around your own home you have learnt to develop a sense of preservation and avoid potential dangers and accident areas. You have become *street wise*. Well, when it comes to travelling into unknown terrain away from the safety of your home environment you have to develop a sense of survival outdoors. You have to become aware of new sounds, smells, colours and a different way of life.

Country people do not have such easy access as town dwellers to all the modern conveniences such as hospitals, ambulances and public transport, so they are very cautious when moving around outdoors. They realize that in the event of an accident or an emergency it could be some time before they get professional treatment. You would do well to remember this yourselves. Once off the beaten track it may not be possible to get

medical help to you immediately, so think about this when planning your route.

Accidents do happen no matter which part of the country you are travelling in. However, many can easily be avoided just by taking simple precautions.

Avoiding accidents: traversing

Most accidents that happen on a hike are nothing more serious than a sprained ankle or a twisted knee, due probably to being over-tired or carrying too heavy a load over uneven ground. You can help yourself to avoid these accidents by walking carefully, particularly on hilly ground in the wet.

Steep grassy slopes and rocky surfaces can be very treacherous and difficult to navigate if they are wet. Often the only way to climb a hill is to *traverse* it from side to side.

Whilst it takes a little longer to reach the top by this method under such conditions it is safer, and can save you a lot of hard work. It is, however, very tiring on the feet over long distances

Traversing

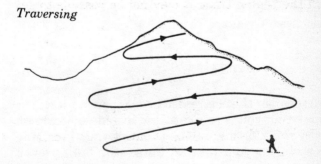

especially as most of the walking is done on the side of the foot as you struggle to retain your balance.

Walking directly downwards on a steep hill can also be very tiring and dangerous if the surface is wet or covered in snow, so it is wise to use the same traversing techniques to descend as you did to climb. A word of warning here, if the slope is very steep and you do not traverse from side to side, continually pushing forward into the toes of your boots will make your feet very sore and the moment that you reach level ground you will find that blisters will begin to appear on the soles of the feet.

This is something that I had to learn from experience — now I'm passing it on to you.

REMEMBER . . . walking directly *up* a steep slope tires the legs, especially the knees.

Walking directly *down* a steep slope makes the backs of your legs and ankles sore.

The bigger the load you carry the quicker you tire.

If you are tired, you're more likely to have an accident. So be careful. Traverse a hill if you need to. Rest if you are tired.

Help yourself

Remember that I stressed how important it was to make out your route card and include several rest and safety stops. In the event of your becoming lost during your hike or, worse still, falling down

and injuring yourself, you know that someone back home has a record of your route and can come to your aid. Perhaps not immediately, but when you fail to show at your final destination they will be able to trace your route and, hopefully, find you. Where this system falls down is when you get lost and wander off your planned route, but even then if you have passed through your stop points and been seen at each one as I explained, your rescuers can localize the area to search.

If rescuers have to turn out to find you, you must try and give them as much help as possible. This you have already done simply by planning your route and noting the stops.

Wearing the right kind of protective clothing is just as important: luminous arm bands, for example, fluorescent clothing, carrying your torch and whistle. See how everything fits into place?

Keeping your boots on

If you should fall and sprain your ankle and you know for certain it is not broken it is wise to keep your boots on as this helps support the ankle. (Generally when you break a bone there is very little swelling around the injury, just a great deal of pain and discolouring due to torn tissues and ligaments and internal bleeding.) If you take your boots off it may be difficult to get them on again later. I personally try to find the nearest cold water, stream or puddle and soak the foot, boot and all, for a while. This helps to ease the swelling, but if the pain gets really bad then obviously I have to remove the boot and strap the foot if possible. Soldiers, especially paratroopers, force the boot back over the strapping to give extra support even if it means having to cut the laces to do so.

You could, of course, make an improvised crutch from anything suitable lying around, and as a last resort use your friend to lean on as you make your way back down to level ground. One thing you must not do is try and carry on; to do so would be silly and dangerous.

Call it a day and rest the foot. There is always another time.

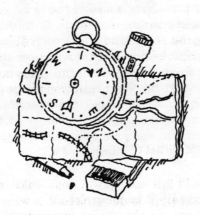

Recognize shock

When someone is injured, perhaps with a dislocated shoulder or a broken limb, they will automatically lapse into a state of shock. Their body is telling them to stop and rest and seek help quickly. Whilst in shock it is very easy to become a hypothermia case as shock quickly uses up body heat, so it is vitally important that you remain with them at this stage – do NOT go rushing off for help. Stay with them and reassure them. If you have a sleeping bag slip them into it and get them out of the COLD . . . WIND . . . WET. If necessary get into the sleeping bag with them so that the heat from your body will give them some warmth.

When someone is in shock their skin becomes cold, pale and clammy, and they may tremble, shiver or sweat profusely even though it is cold. Once normal breathing returns then you can think about going for help. Use your senses, listen for steady breathing, and feel the skin around the face or wrists to see if warmth is returning. Do not be afraid to talk to them even though they may be unconscious. Nature will take its course, and as soon as it wants to send them to sleep it will. Then you can start thinking about going for help. Only you can make that decision. I personally have always made absolutely sure that an injured person was safe and comfortable (to the best of my ability) before I set off.

Reassuring a friend – and yourself

If your friend is bleeding badly you will have to try and stop the loss of blood, and if they have fallen in such a way that it is impossible to move them, you may have to build some form of protection from the wet and wind. In any event you will have lots of decisions to make quickly. Keep calm, move slowly and deliberately and keep talking, even if you know your friend cannot hear you. It is a safety valve for you. It helps steady the nerves.

Television programmes about operations are shown every so often. Next time you watch one, note how the surgeon performing the operation talks all the time. It is to tell everyone else in the operating theatre what is going on, but it also helps to calm the surgeon's nerves, because even experts get nervous when under pressure.

Going for help

Take your torch, whistle, compass and map with you, but leave your friend's out and within easy reach. Note the time you set off, and leave a

Position an injured person in a flat, sheltered spot, easily seen by rescuers

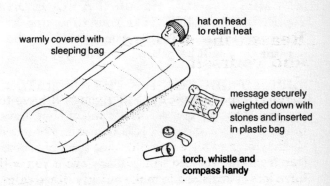

hat on head
to retain heat

warmly covered with
sleeping bag

message securely
weighted down with
stones and inserted
in plastic bag

torch, whistle and
compass handy

written message with your friend stating where you have gone and when you left. Include in your message a brief account of how the accident happened and leave *both* your names. This helps the rescuers when they arrive. Remember you may be exhausted when you eventually find help and on your instructions they have to take charge, so they will be grateful for any information you can assist them with.

Every second counts when seeking help but do not jeopardize your own safety. Control your panic as best you can. The sooner you get your friend proper medical treatment the safer it is for everyone. Out there alone, perhaps slipping into a state of hypothermia, he or she is depending on you.

The first human habitation you come across, go to it. If they have a telephone they can call out the rescue teams. However, if you come across a telephone before you see anyone, *you* call up the emergency services. Simply ring 999 and take it from there.

REMEMBER . . . YOU ARE JUST A VOICE ON THE END OF A LINE. Take your time, and be guided by them. Even as you speak to the operator they will be getting help for you.

DON'T FORGET TO GIVE THE OPERATOR *BOTH* YOUR NAMES AND FULL DETAILS OF WHERE YOU ARE.

7

Living rough ... surviving in an emergency

The worst thing that could happen to you in isolated countryside (other than having a nasty accident) is that you become separated from your equipment.

As strange as it may seem, it is very easy to do just that. Many campers and hikers have removed their rucksacks from their backs to take a rest and wandered away to observe the view, or accidentally knocked their rucksack over a cliff. Some have even left their rucksacks out as markers for friends coming up behind only to lose them as rolling mist silently enshrouded the hills. I even know of one who left his rucksack behind on a bus and yet foolishly went ahead with the walk. Fortunately he was lucky, the weather was kind to him, but he took a terrible risk, and you must never do anything silly like this. However, accidents do happen and when they do you must be prepared for them.

Soldiers learn very quickly that to become separated from their equipment could cost them their lives, so they are trained to survive, to live off the land, and during training they are taught four very important watchwords ... INSPECTION ... PROTECTION ... LOCATION ... FOOD. These apply to you if you too want to survive. Remember, soldiers do it for real, so why don't we learn from the experts.

Let's assume that the worst has happened. You're completely lost, high up in the hills in open countryside. Your equipment has vanished, it is getting dark, and you are facing up to a night of living rough while you wait for help to arrive.

Inspection

The moment that you realize you are in a survival situation, STOP whatever you are doing and sit down. Give yourself time to think. If you want to, try shouting. It helps to ease tension. If you feel like crying, cry. Once that is over you can settle into a survival routine. Next take everything out of your pockets and lay it on the ground in front of you. Examine each item and see if it can be used to help your situation.

Coins, for instance, can be rubbed down to make a sharp cutting edge, used as fishing weights, spread on the ground as a marker signal, or you could use a coin to scratch messages on rocks. Your handkerchief can act as a bandage, water filter, signal flag, fishing net, or as a face visor against snow glare or heat stroke. A handkerchief can be used to leave messages on and, torn into strips, will make rope or fishing line. Handkerchiefs also make excellent slings in an emergency, and, wrapped around the fingers, they help to keep out the cold and prevent frostbite. You can even draw yourself a rough map on your handkerchief. IMPROVISATION IS THE NAME OF THE GAME.

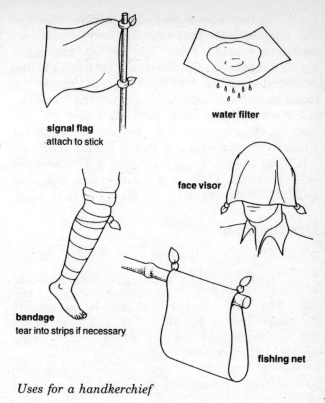

signal flag
attach to stick

water filter

face visor

bandage
tear into strips if necessary

fishing net

Uses for a handkerchief

Remember your survival kit and how you packed everything away in a matchbox in your pocket . . . NOT IN YOUR RUCKSACK . . . for just an emergency. Well now that emergency is here and you will see how practical it is.

You now have matches to light your fire with, and pencil and paper to leave messages, tin foil, and fishing line to make a cooker, and, if you have

water, an Oxo cube to make a hot drink. I bet you
are pleased now that you decided to take my
advice and make a survival kit up. Having it
handy could mean the difference between life and
death. Remember how I explained that everything must have a multiple use, well now you can
see if everything does work, and test out the
home-made compass with the pin. What better
chance will you ever get to put it into practice?

It is up to you to use whatever is available for
your survival. Once you have completed your
INSPECTION you can move on to the next stage.

Protection

Knowing now that the COLD . . . WET . . . WIND
are three potential killers, it is important to try
and protect yourself from them as soon as possible. You have already been wandering around
for hours looking for help. Now you have to get
yourself organized and prepare for a night living
rough. Let's assume that no help is likely to
appear at least until tomorrow morning, so the
first priority for now is to find or make some kind
of shelter.

You might come across a small cave or rock
overhang, even a fallen tree, all of which will
make a shelter for the night, or you could be
unlucky and find nothing suitable. If that is the
case, then you will have to set about making your
own shelter. Watch the animals on the hills. They
know where the best places are. If it is still
daylight see if you can spot their resting places.
Even a small indentation in the ground is better
than sitting out in the open.

As the cold night air creeps in, the earth will begin to cool, and high on the hills the temperature will drop dramatically. If the wind is strong it will steal away your precious body heat, so it is important to get down off the skyline as quickly as possible. If the ground beneath you is dry, take off your jacket and wear it like a blanket. This helps to trap warm air and stops it from escaping. If your jacket has a hood, use it — a great deal of your body heat is lost if the head is left exposed to the cold and wind. Remember to draw your feet up under you and to tuck your hands beneath your jacket. Turn to face the wind. DO NOT turn your back to it as the large area exposed is difficult to keep warm. Accept that you are in for a cold, miserable night and that it is very unlikely that you will get any sleep at all.

Wash your face

During the early hours of the morning it will become extremely cold and you may feel like getting up and moving around to try and get warm. This is not a wise thing to do as you could easily stumble over a rock or, worse, fall over a ledge and hurt yourself. The safest thing to do is to try and get some rest, even if it means scraping some of the earth away from beneath you to make your bed more comfortable.

As you lie there all kinds of thoughts will be going through your head. This is natural. Again it is your body telling you that something is wrong and you must try to do something about it, so take advantage of not being able to sleep and try to work out a plan of what you will do as soon as it gets light. This will help you to settle down and hopefully get some rest. Providing it does not rain or snow you will come to no real harm.

Just before dawn as the sun begins to rise you can expect a heavy dew. This will chill you even more, but do not worry, as daylight creeps across the sky you will soon be up and about.

In the cold dawn air visibility is often very good, so as soon as you feel able, get up and shake yourself out. A few brisk exercises will soon have you feeling better. If you have anything in the way of food or sweets in your pocket, eat some. If there is any fresh water, drink some of that, but take care . . . . Remember you are on high ground and all water will be very cold. Take just a sip to begin with, swill out your mouth first and then drink more later. If there is any to spare splash a bit on your face. A little hygiene is a great morale booster.

Making a shelter

Depending on the weather, sometimes it is wiser to remain where you are (rather than blunder around) and hope that the rescue team will find you. Take advantage of any daylight to get yourself organized, especially if you think you will have to spend another evening there.

Collect stones and grass, even moss and peat. Form them into a small circular wall shelter strong enough to keep out the driving wind. If there are any sticks available use these to make a roof and cover them with lots of grass, heather or bracken. Do not forget to pack some grass and heather inside the shelter to lie on. Insulation from the damp earth is very important. The more you pack in, the warmer it will be, and whilst you are working, put out a few marker signs for any rescuers to spot. You will get warm as you work, so take off one of your inner garments and try to fasten it to something that will make a flag. If the weather is not too bad you could spread your waterproof out on a nearby rock – anything to

Circular stone shelter

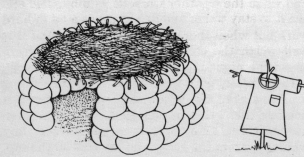

attract attention. But I do stress that you should only remove any garments if the weather is suitable and you feel it is safe to do so.

Do your work during the morning. In the afternoon rest, even sleep, if you feel tired. Hang out any clothes to dry and, as you rest, your marker signals will be working for you. Come the evening, you should be able to get a good night's sleep.

REMEMBER . . . before you decide to build your shelter choose a good spot. There is no point in putting out marker signals if when the rescuers arrive they cannot find you.

A grass shelter

This is a second type of shelter, useful where fewer materials are available. Soldiers are taught how to build them, and you can easily do so too. First, gather grass, bracken and heather into a big pile. Then jump up and down on it to squash it as tightly as you can so that it makes a very firm base. Collect another lot and pile this on top of the first until you have a good heap, ideally as tall as yourself. This is a true survival shelter, and when the weather worsens, climb inside and use it to stay warm and dry. It takes a lot of hard work but when there is nothing else around it is well worth the effort, especially if you have to spend the night in the open.

To get really good insulation, do not just throw it all in a heap. Set it down in layers: grass, then heather, then bracken, repeated several times. To keep out the rain, pull moss, if there is any available, from the rocks and lay this on the top.

Grass and bracken shelter

If there is no moss, try a few grass sods. Once you have made your shelter and you are snugly tucked up inside you will be amazed how comfortable it can be.

A couple of safety warnings here. Take care when pulling up bracken as it can be very sharp. In the country it is known as nature's razor blades. Better to kick it loose with your feet first before collecting it.

Another safety tip: do remember that the rescue teams will be out searching for you and if you are fast asleep inside your shelter they may not be able to spot you easily. So do not forget to leave some kind of a signal marker, otherwise they may walk right past you.

Shelter in the snow

Surviving when there is snow on the ground is not all that different from the rest of the year.

You can still use the bracken and heather to make a base, but this time you have an added bonus: snow, and probably lots of it, which means you can build yourself a survival shelter.

Snow makes a very good insulator from the COLD . . . WET . . . WIND, and is often much easier to work with than other building materials. What you want to try and do is to find a place where the snow has built up against a rock face or filled in a ground hollow. This way you will not have to go searching for building materials, you simply burrow into it. For obvious reasons you have to be doubly cautious about hypothermia conditions when working with snow. It is going to be much colder, especially for your hands and feet, and you must be careful not to overwork and cause excessive sweating. You know how important it is to retain your body heat, so you must work cautiously.

If you are lucky enough to find a rock overhang where the snow has gathered deeply then you are in luck. Now all you have to do is to scoop out a snow cave. Keep the snow that you remove, and

Snow cave

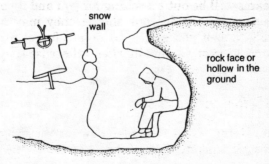

snow wall

rock face or hollow in the ground

roll it into balls. You can use them to make a wind-break around your snow cave entrance.

If you find that your fingers are getting cold, remove the linings from your pockets and use these as gloves. As soon as you feel your fingers beginning to sting, stop and warm them. Tuck them inside your jacket beneath your armpits. If you do want to rub them do so gently until the stinging goes.

A snow house

You could, if you thought you were capable of doing so, build yourself a small igloo. This is not as big a task as you might think. If the snow is deep enough and there are no deep drifts to burrow into, an igloo could save your life.

Start by rolling the snow into balls about the size of a football. Place these in a circle large

Igloo

vent hole at top

entrance
tunnel

enough for you to sit in comfortably with your
legs stretched out in front of you. The base circle
needs to be fairly strong and thick so you may
have to make a double circle. Pack loose snow
between each layer of balls and just keep building
upwards, gently leaning the walls in as you do so.
Smooth the inside of the walls off with your hands
and remove any surplus loose snow from inside as
it quickly melts, and makes everything soggy.

If you find difficulty in sealing the opening at
the top, scratch beneath the surface of the snow
and pull up handfuls of grass and bracken or
heather and lay this across. Then very gently
cover it with soft snow until you have built
yourself a reasonably solid roof. If you can reach
from the outside, smooth the roof off, otherwise if
the wind gets up it will blow the snow away and
leave you with a gaping hole.

Remember to insulate your body from the cold
earth. Search for bracken, heather, etc. To stop
heat escaping, build yourself a small entrance
tunnel.

All this will take time and patience, so work
slowly and try to avoid sweating. When you get
tired STOP AND REST, and keep out of the wind.
Do not forget to leave your marker flags showing
while you rest inside. If you have no markers,
build a couple of snowmen where they will be
easily seen – on a hill-top, for example.

Leaving markers

If you decide not to rest during the afternoon after
you've made your shelter, you could try a little
exploration, providing the weather is clear and

you feel up to it. But do remember to mark your trail so that you can get back safely and do not forget to leave some kind of a message just in case anyone should come whilst you are away.

At the most you should be away no more than half an hour. Return, rest a few minutes and go exploring in another direction. If time allows do this three or four times, but always keep your shelter and markers in view.

Why do you do this? Well you might just be lucky and spot the search team or some other walkers. It also occupies your mind and enables you to study in detail the terrain and if possible judge from which direction the rescue team may come.

REMEMBER ... during your initial planning you marked down on your map and route card where the mountain rescue centres were situated. It was part of your safety escape route.

On your brief walkabouts try to remain on the skyline as much as possible and avoid climbing down into gulleys and river beds. Keep warm and dry. You might have to spend another night on the hills.

Lighting a fire

Lighting a fire high in the hills is not difficult. The problem comes when you want to keep it going. Heather, bracken and grass burn quickly when dry, but when wet are very difficult to set alight.

A fire, like the rest of your survival aids, must serve a multiple role. Choose a suitable place to

grass, bracken etc.
ready to burn

fire

rock face

stones or logs at base
to protect and contain fire

sticks for evening burning

dry sheltered ground

Siting a fire

site it. Somewhere you can get most benefit from
the heat . . . preferably close to a rock face where
the heat can be reflected back towards you and
not be blown away. To start with keep it small
and manageable. You do not want to be rushing
around all the time trying to find tinder to keep
it going. Keep any wood or twigs for the evening,
and during the day burn dry grass and bracken.
They are easy to find and give off lots of thick
smoke needed to signal with. Unfortunately
grass, bracken and heather do not give off a great
deal of heat unless they are burnt in very large
quantities.

Making a twirl

To make the grass and bracken last longer twist
it lightly together into what country folk call
twirls. Many, many years ago hill farmers and
crofters used to do this all the time, as coal and
wood were very expensive. Remember what I said
about bracken being very sharp – take care when
twisting it. Mix the heather and grass into one
twirl and you will find that it burns better.

A twirl pyramid

When you have made sufficient twirls lay about half a dozen down on the ground alongside each other to form a little platform. The rest you stand upright to make a pyramid. Take one of the matches from your survival kit and also your spare match striker. Hold them as close to the fire twirls as you can, making sure that the match does not blow out. Light your fire and gently feed fresh twirls to it as it grows. If you want to make a lot of smoke to signal with, try burning just dry grass without making it into twirls.

Remember if the ground is covered with snow, you want as much smoke as you can make, so the greener the foliage and grass, the better.

Location

If you forgot to tie your compass and whistle around your neck as I suggested earlier, you will probably have no idea in which direction you are facing. If you have got your survival kit you can make yourself a matchstick and pin survival compass (as described on page 31).

There are several other ways to find north. Use as many as you can to check your direction.

Finding north at night

Just because you are not travelling at night, it does not mean that you sit idle. All the time you are awake you must be thinking survival. For instance, providing the night sky is clear, it is possible to find north by following the stars.

Look for a group of stars known as the Great Plough, Dipper, or Ursa Major (all names for the same group). It is easy to recognize and this is the shape to look for.

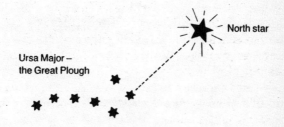

Finding north by the stars

To find the North Star simply follow a straight line using the two bottom stars as a guide until you come to a very bright star — the same star, it is said, that the three wise men followed to find Jesus. If you measure five times the distance between the two bottom stars of the Plough you will come to this bright North Star. As its name suggests, it will give you a constant north point. Once you have located it put out a land marker. When you awake in the morning you will immediately be able to see in which direction north lies.

Wristwatch compass

You can use your wristwatch as a compass too. Simply point the hour hand of the watch at the sun. The most accurate way is to hold the watch flat in your hand. Later, when you become more experienced, you can leave it on your wrist. Now halve the distance between the hour-hand and twelve noon as shown.

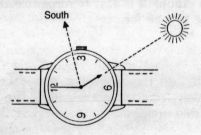

Finding south using a wristwatch

This will give you a north-south line. But remember that this only works when you are in the northern hemisphere, and on Greenwich Mean Time.

If you want to find south using your watch on British Summer Time follow the same procedure as before, only this time halve the distance between one o'clock and the hour hand.

Sun dial

If you haven't got a wristwatch, you can make a sun dial, both to tell the time, and to find north. In some parts of the world this is known as the shadow stick method.

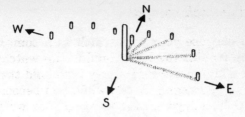

Shadow stick sundial

Choose a level piece of ground cleared of shrubs, stones, etc. Find a small stick about 8–12 ins (20–30cm) long, preferably nice and straight. At a push a pencil or ball point pen will do. Press the stick into the ground so that the sun casts a shadow from it. At the end of the shadow place another small stick. This is your first marker.

As the sun rises and sets the shadows cast by the stick become shorter and longer. As they do, place other smaller sticks or stones at the end of each shadow. At midday, the sun will be at its highest point so the shadows will be at their shortest. At midday, the sun is in the south, so this shortest shadow will be pointing north.

Land compass

If you've found north by some of these methods, and your results (roughly) agree, you can make yourself a land compass. This is simply a pile of sticks or rocks set out a few metres away from your camp on each of the four directional points of the compass . . . NORTH . . . SOUTH . . . EAST . . . WEST. A land compass is an excellent survival aid because it allows you to wander

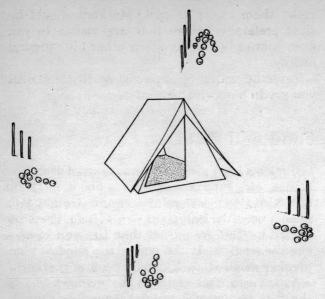

A land compass, constructed from sticks and stones

further afield from your camp site in safety. If you should get lost you simply find your way back by following the compass markers.

This system is still widely used today by many nomadic peoples and has saved thousands of lives, mine included. Many times when I have been crossing the deserts and bush lands of the world as an explorer I have relied on my marker sticks to guide me safely back to camp. People who live in jungles mark trees, and the Australian Aborigines use small fires burning on top of distant hills. If you want to, you can build scarecrows on the nearby horizon or put tufts of grass or strips of cloth on your marker flags to make them easier to spot. Markers should be sited preferably where they are visible to you from your camp and from any other high ground nearby.

Never be scared of improvising. REMEMBER you are in a survival situation.

Food and drink

Fiddle heads and other delicacies

All this hard work is going to take a lot of effort on your part. Nothing comes easy in a survival situation. You have to work that little bit harder if you want to live.

To enable you to work your body will require energy. You get energy from food and drink, and where do we get food and drink up there? Well, during the winter many new edible plants will be lying dormant just beneath the ground waiting for spring and the warm weather, so if you very gently scoop away the snow and earth you will find lots of new shoots just waiting to be picked. Take bracken shoots for instance: they are called fiddle heads because they look like the top of a fiddle. They are very sweet, need no cooking and can be eaten raw.

Fresh moorland reed shoots can also be eaten, and the small leaves of bilberries and heather. On many moorlands and mountains you will find a small tree growing with bright red berries on it. This is called a mountain ash or rowan tree. The berries are used to make jam and wine, and can be eaten raw but not in large quantities as they

may make you sick. The little black bilberries on
the other hand are very nutritious and easy to
find amongst the heather.

WARNING . . . you should *only* taste something
that you do not recognize if there is no other
source of food available and you are desperate.

REMEMBER . . . it is water (liquids) that the body
will need urgently. Most people, you included, can
survive off your body fat for a week or so without
too much trouble. Without water you will only
last a few days. However, if there is food available, eat it. Better for it to be inside you making
energy than sitting there.

Water

Water is your number one priority in any survival situation. Without it you die. It is as simple
as that.

Water helps lubricate the flow of blood through
the body and helps to regulate the body
temperature. Normally in cold conditions we tend
to drink less because we do not perspire as much,
but in your situation, especially when you have
been working hard, it is very important to
replenish the body's water supply as soon as
possible.

All fresh rain water can be drunk at source
without the need for any purification, providing it
is collected in a clean container. Fresh snow and
ice (not salt water ice) can be melted down and
drunk. To get the best snow, scrape away the top
inch (3cm) and remove the lower fall. Hold this in

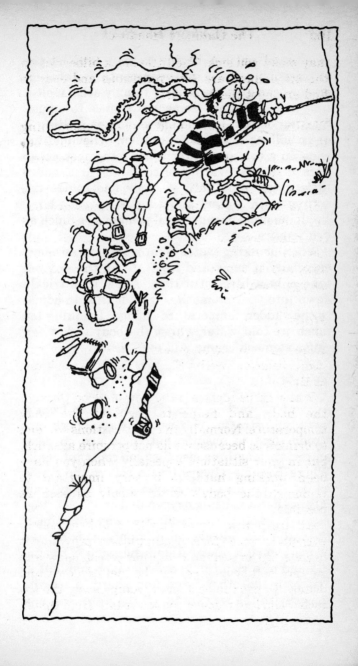

your hand until it begins to melt, and let the water dribble slowly into your mouth. Sucking ice or snow can give you a nasty tummy ache: melt it first and give your stomach a chance to adjust. Sucking on cold ice and snow without melting it down will make you even thirstier. When melting snow in a container over a fire remember *not to pack it tightly*. Warm the container first, add a little snow, wait until it melts and covers the bottom with water, and then keep on adding small amounts of snow until you have as much as you require.

When drinking water from mountain streams, especially if snow and frost are on the ground, take only a little at a time. Allow it to trickle down into your stomach to give it time to adjust to the sudden temperature change. Drinking too much ice-cold water whilst the body is hot can cause stomach cramp and even death.

Test first

A word of warning when taking water from a mountain stream or river. Always check upstream first to ensure that there are no dead animals or anything else that can contaminate it. Where possible always try to collect the water whilst it is cascading over a rock or log. This means that it is being oxygenated and is not stagnant. A simple but very effective way of testing if the water has any chemical impurities is to take a small amount of wax from inside your ear using the end of a clean finger. Scoop up a handful of water in the other hand and gently place the finger with the wax into it. If the water has any

chemical impurities, when it comes into contact
with the wax it will immediately take on a colour
spectrum, like a rainbow.

Why? Because . . . WATER AND WAX DO NOT
MIX.

If the water is clear (and most mountain water
is) the wax particles will sink to the bottom of the
water in your hand and gleam white.

REMEMBER, this is a basic water test and
should only be used in emergency survival situations or when you have no other means of
testing. It is better to treat the water with steriliz-
ing tablets if you have them, or boil it.

On your way again

You have your markers out, a shelter to protect
you from the COLD . . . WET . . . WIND, a fire
going *(no matter how small)*. But you still cannot
relax and must consider the possibility of not
being found by the rescue team. Maybe you will
have to make your own way back to safety. The
less time you spend in a survival situation the
better.

An early start

Having carried out many inspections of the
surrounding area you should now be familiar
with it, and, using your survival compass, you
should have worked out a possible route back to
safety.

You have a crude map that you made from your

handkerchief or a piece of paper from your survival kit, all your clothes are dry, and you even managed to make yourself a hot drink of Oxo from your survival kit. Now it is time to move on.

Leaving your markers out, and a message inside your shelter telling where you have gone, you can set off. Try to leave early in the morning. The more daylight you have to travel in the better. If visibility is good, keep a look out for any recognizable landmarks and slowly make your way down to them.

Running water finds its way to lower ground, so all running water must be considered as a route source. Do not walk too close to any streams or rivers especially when they are fast flowing. Keep them in view and in earshot. Where possible avoid crossing and recrossing. This makes it difficult for anyone to follow you.

Leave a trail

As you make your way down to safety you must be extra wary of accidents. Try to avoid walking on slippery rocks or close to steep ridges, especially if the wind is blowing hard. If it is raining and blowing your energy will be seeping away quickly, so keep within your limits. If you have to make detours around large objects or wide streams, try to mark a point on the opposite side and get back on to your route when you cross.

Leave a few marker arrows on stones or rocks using the chalk from your survival kit. Make sure that you allow for stops and rest periods as you descend.

If you have to cross any marshy ground, step on the tufts of grass rather than walking in the water, and if by the time midday arrives you are still not safely down, prepare to spend another night in the hills, and keep an eye open for a possible camp site. As you descend the wind and cold will not be as fierce so you should have an easier journey. Allow yourself time to prepare a shelter, light a fire, collect tinder and hopefully find some food. Keep planning ahead all the time.

Think survival and you will survive.

When you eventually do get down to safety do not forget that you started off with a friend and naturally you will want to know if he/she is safe.

Let the police know you are back as they will be working closely with any search teams out looking for you. Many times I have been out on a rescue and the people we were searching for simply came down off the hills and went back home without informing anyone.

Finally, it goes without saying

TELEPHONE YOUR PARENTS IMMEDIATELY

Do not think for one moment that all your adventures will end up in a survival situation. On the contrary, providing you follow the guidelines I have set out for your planning and preparation you should have no trouble at all, and even if you are unlucky enough to find yourself in such a situation you now know how to deal with it.

REMEMBER YOUR SURVIVAL RULES INSPECTION . . . PROTECTION . . . LOCATION . . . FOOD

Good planning and preparation will not only make your adventure more enjoyable but will also keep you alive.

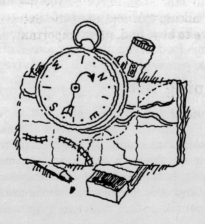

8
Camping

Now that you know how to plan a simple hiking holiday, and what to do to protect yourself should you be unfortunate enough to get lost, or separated from your equipment, let's go one step further and plan a weekend's camping.

Campers prefer sleeping outdoors rather than returning home each evening, and to enable them to do this in safety and comfort they have to take with them extra outdoor equipment, much of it specialized, such as a tent, sleeping bag and cooking stove. It therefore follows that the planning and preparation for a camping trip is similar to your hiking adventure, with a few extras.

Compare the camping planning list I have done to your hiking list and note the extra items you will have to buy, and, more important, carry with you.

Planning list
Equipment

Tent, clothing, cooking utensils, knife, fork, spoon, mug, sleeping bag, compass, maps, torch with spare batteries and bulb, whistles, first aid box, waterproofs, rucksack, radio/spare batteries, string, pencil, paper, matches, plimsolls.

Safety

Telephone numbers: Mum/Dad/neighbour, camp site owner, local police. Correct equipment.

Distance

An area where in an emergency you can easily be found or walk away from.

Cost

Money for travel, campsite fees, purchasing stores and equipment, telephone calls, possible emergencies, visits to cafés and museums, etc. Buy a *return* ticket when you set out.

Location

An area that you know is suitable to your requirements and that you will feel safe in. CONFIRM CAMPSITE BOOKING IN WRITING.

Route

Perfect your map reading skills, and practise basic navigation (using the stars, sun etc, as well as your compass). Plan your daily walks, including safety exits.

Choosing a tent

Don't forget to invite Mum and Dad to go along to the shop with you, because this time you will have to spend a lot more money than you did on your hiking equipment, and you will need an adult's guidance.

As with most outdoor equipment there is a great variety to choose from and it is a buyer's market so do not be pressured into buying something that is not suitable. Camping equipment can be very expensive. Ideally your tent should have both a sewn-in groundsheet and an inner lining.

Before you buy, ask the shop owner to let you put a couple of sleeping bags inside. This will give you some idea of how much space you and your friend will have.

Remember it is only for sleeping in, so do not buy something that is big and bulky. Weight is very important when you have to carry your tent over long distances. Make sure that it is waterproof, that it complies with international rescue colours, and, if possible, is made of fireproof material. Modern tents now have unbreakable pegs and folding glass fibre poles as well as non-

A tent with an inner lining and sewn-in groundsheet gives you extra protection against the cold, wet and wind

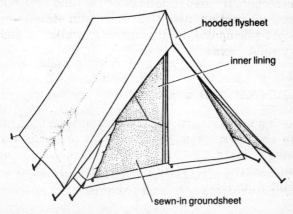

hooded flysheet

inner lining

sewn-in groundsheet

stick zips and velcro fasteners (essential for a quick exit in an emergency).

When you have purchased your tent, practise putting it up in the garden and if possible spend a few nights in it before you set off on your camping trip.

A good survival skill is to erect the tent in the dark. You never know when you may have to do it for real, and practice makes perfect.

Your sleeping bag

Choosing the right kind of sleeping bag is equally important as choosing your tent. Many sleeping bags sold to young, inexperienced campers are unsuitable and often dangerous. Remember the purpose of the sleeping bag is to keep you warm, safe and dry, so it is essential to make sure that it complies with certain safety standards. Ideally it should be made of fireproof material and have a waterproof base. It should be fitted with a *full length* non-stick zip or velcro fastener and, if your pocket will stand it, filled with down feathers. Many campers argue that a waterproof base is not necessary today as it is possible to buy a carry-mat. This is a long strip of flexible foam, very light, which rolls up tightly to be carried on the top of your rucksack. A good survival tip to remember when choosing your sleeping bag is that the higher you camp in the hills the colder it gets, so a well filled sleeping bag is essential for comfort.

I personally always use an ex-military one. It is strong, robust, easy to pack, and not as expensive

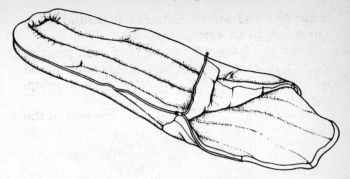

Your sleeping bag should have a full-length zip or Velcro fastener

as many of the modern ones on today's market.

Before you buy your sleeping bag make sure that you can get inside it with your clothes ON.

This is very important, as many cheap sleeping bags restrict your movement as you toss and turn during the night. In an emergency you may need to get out of it quickly.

Camping stoves

As this is your first camping trip do not make the mistake of spending a lot of money on a bulky camping stove. At the most you will only be cooking a couple of meals on it, so why pay out a great deal for it. Once you begin to camp further afield then you can afford to buy one of the expensive models.

A basic Calor Gaz stove will serve your needs, it is easy to carry, and packs away neatly. Spares are easily obtainable and most camp site shops stock various gaz canisters.

I DO NOT RECOMMEND PETROL OR SOLID FUEL STOVES

Petrol stoves are best suited to experienced campers such as a family group. Solid fuel is suitable for those who like to camp off the beaten track. The bigger the stove, the more fuel you will have to carry.

Make sure that your stove is fitted with a firm, wide base. Cooking out in the wilds can be a little hazardous sometimes, but NEVER . . . NEVER attempt to cook inside your tent. It is stupid and dangerous.

Pots and pans

It is not necessary to purchase a lot of cooking utensils at this stage. You may have to buy a tin plate and mug, but you could take a knife, fork and spoon set from your home (check with your parents first though).

If you have enough money, you could purchase a set of aluminium mess tins. They can act as cooking pans, storage containers and plates. Be sure to get a set with lids fitted: they help to keep your food hot, prevent spillages, speed up your cooking time, and can save on fuel. If your money will not run to a set of aluminium plates you could take a plastic one, but you will still need something metal to cook in.

REMEMBER . . . consider weight and bulk before you buy.

Checking and preparing

The rest of your equipment is straightforward and as you see, most of it you will already have purchased for your hiking trip. Once you have everything together, make sure you practise using it in the safety of your back garden or nearby park. This way if there is anything wrong with any of the items you will have time to replace it. If you look again at the planning list on pages 107–8 you will notice that there are six separate headings. Go through each one of these very carefully, ticking off each item as you check it. Make sure that you have spare batteries and bulbs for your torch, and that your first aid pack is complete. Double check all your telephone numbers, and your site booking.

Check that the campsite owner knows when you will be arriving and that your booking is confirmed. Note down the telephone number and leave a copy for your parents. REMEMBER, ONLY A FOOL GOES CAMPING ALONE.

As this is your first camping trip use one of the registered camping sites. Not only will you be safer, but you can use the site as a permanent base to go exploring from.

Leaving your tent and all your equipment out in the wilds whilst you wander around is not a wise thing to do. Remember those stories of people who became separated from their rucksacks whilst out hiking?

PLAY SAFE . . . use the experiences of others.

Choosing your pitch

When you arrive at the camp site it is important to choose a good location. Stay away from trees or alongside fences. If there are animals in the field they tend to use these areas for resting and many an inexperienced camper has been rudely awoken during the early hours of the morning to find his tent trodden on by a nosy cow or a grazing sheep.

Avoid pitching your tent close to streams, steep cliffs or banks. During a storm or heavy mist it could be dangerous and will almost certainly be a lot colder, especially by a river. Ask the site owner to choose a place for you, and if you feel it is not suitable, say so. It is no good complaining in the middle the night because you keep slipping down to the bottom of your tent, having pitched it on a slope.

If you have to fasten your guy ropes to anything other than a tent peg make sure that it does not get in anyone else's way. Washing lines across a footpath can lead to a nasty confrontation with any unfortunate camper who happens to come across them whilst making their way to the toilet during the night, and campers arriving on a motor cycle could find themselves being decapitated.

If you are a light sleeper avoid pitching your tent close to the car park or latrines, and never put your tent between two others. If you have to, make sure that they have not gone out for the day in the car. You could be in their parking space, and if they return home late at night – 'POW'.

9

Ideas for outdoors holidays

Just because you are on a camping holiday it does not mean that you are restricted to one outdoor activity. Thousands of campers take the opportunity to try rock climbing, a little inshore dinghy sailing, canoeing or pony trekking.

Whatever the adventure, remember that it will cost extra money, and the more specialized the activity the more you will have to pay.

Apply the same rules as you did when planning your hiking trip. Do not be too ambitious. Pony trekking, for instance, may sound great but after a few hours riding across the country, it could leave you very stiff for a couple of days. Try things in moderation. Many outdoor activity centres may require you to take out a separate insurance indemnity before taking part, so check that the centre is insured before you sign up.

Rock climbing and canoeing require specialized equipment on which your life will depend. Check with the campsite owner or nearest Tourist Information Centre that the centre is reputable.

REMEMBER having a sign above a door does not signify that all is well. If you have any doubts at all ask the local Mountain Rescue Centre or Police Station. They know who is and is not genuine.

If you do intend to try out a new activity it might be wise to do a little pre-training back at your home first.

Canoeing requires that you go through a thorough build-up of safety skills before you can venture out on an expedition and, because there is a danger the canoe will capsize, it is essential that you can swim. So why not go along to your local swimming baths for some fitness training.

Climbing can be hard on your hands and legs, so a little weight lifting, jogging and hill walking will help to ease any stiffness.

Many riding schools insist on spending the first lesson (irrespective of whether you can ride or not) trotting round a paddock, doing what they call familiarizing yourself with your pony. You could be paying anything from £8 to £25 per hour for this – so it can be very expensive before you even manage to get out and about.

Now you can see why I recommend that you buy a return ticket before you set off. If you do happen to overspend you will at least have your fare home. It is all to do with your planning and preparation.

Extra outdoor activities are great, but they need to be planned for.

An excellent way to spend a few hours without running through too much of your money is to visit local museums, castles, sports centres, or zoos. You can get details either from the local Tourist Information Centre, from campsite offices, police stations, or from your parents' AA or RAC information bureau. I personally have spent many pleasant hours wandering around old ruins and buildings, relaxing before returning to my tent. It is a very good way of finding out about local history.

If you are lucky, a local gala day or village fête may be on. They are nearly always well worth a visit, especially if you come from a town. Country fêtes and galas offer superb entertainment for everyone and are excellent value for money.

Providing that it is not too expensive and fits in with your schedule, try a guided bus tour. These can be very informative, but do make sure that they get you back in time to return to your campsite safely. Many return after dark.

10

Tracking made easy

As a small boy, I never wanted to become a famous pilot or train driver like other kids when I grew up. From the moment I saw my first cowboys and Indians film I knew that I wanted to be a professional tracker.

I wanted to follow the trails of wild animals through the dense steamy jungles, and track after baddies across the vast deserts and prairies of the world.

At every opportunity I would be off to the nearest park or woods to practise, and when I eventually went into the armed services I used my tracking skills there. Sometimes it helped to save not only my life but others', and since

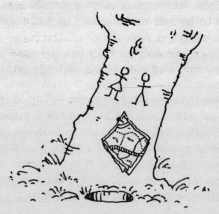

leaving the army, I have on many occasions been asked by both the police (of many countries) and various armed services to help track down criminals and people lost on the moors and mountains.

Tracking is great fun and easy to learn. In just a few minutes you too can be following trails like the Indians in the cowboy films. Tracking teaches you to respect nature, and most trackers are good naturalists and conservationists.

Careful now!

Tracking allows you to get very close to nature and most people who practise tracking do not in any way harm or disturb the wild life.

Before you begin tracking it is important to remember a couple of basic survival rules. Firstly, never go tracking alone, or attempt to track at night, and secondly, know your limits. Long tracks can be very tiring and should be done in stages. Remember most animals and humans prefer to be left undisturbed so take care.

Following a person's trail whilst he or she is out walking could end up with you accused of being a peeping tom and you might end up getting a thick ear.

Especially when you are learning, it is best to practise on your mum or dad, or a friend. Later, as you get more experienced, perhaps you could offer to use your expertise in helping to find someone who may be lost.

When following an animal's trail there are certain precautions you must take. Remember most

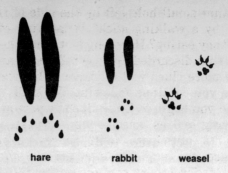

hare   **rabbit**   **weasel**

Some animal footprints

animals prefer to be left alone and do not take kindly to being disturbed, especially if they have young with them or they are in the process of eating. So beware, they could end up attacking you. It is important that you do practise tracking both humans and animals and learn the difference between the trails they leave. Humans when out walking tend to stay in straight lines and leave very specific signs for you to follow: footprints, discarded fruit, sweet wrappings, cast-off clothing and even messges. Animals, on the other hand, move in a more erratic way, and leave fewer signs.

Reading the signs

Visual signs left by humans can be very interesting to decode. Soon you will discover that tracking is very much like being a NATURE DETECTIVE.

For instance, why did the two footprints come together then suddenly swing off to the right?

Was that small hole left by the side of the print made by a walking stick? What kind of sweets were they eating? How long is it since they threw away that discarded apple core? These and many many more clues will all have to be worked out before you continue following the trail.

Soon you begin to think like the person you are following and as you get more experienced you begin to anticipate their moves. Scouts, for instance, are taught to leave certain signs along the trail for others coming up behind them to interpret. A bit like leaving clues.

Following an animal's trail can be just as interesting. For instance, animals with hooves tend to be grazers, and nibble and chew at the foliage as the wander, so they often appear very docile and easy to approach. Meat eaters, carnivores, on the other hand generally have very sharp claws and teeth, and because they have to hunt for their food they are very nervous and mistrusting, especially when cornered, and would not hesitate to attack you. So obviously you do not put yourself in a position where they will turn on you.

REMEMBER tracking is fun. It is not a battle between you and the animals. Treat the animals you are tracking with the respect they deserve. Observe them, study them, and above all learn from them.

Starting out

To begin tracking you need nothing more than a few small sticks, about 10 ins (25cm) long, some

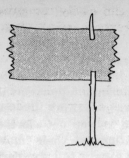

A tracking flag

old sheets of newspaper to make your flags with, and a pencil and a notepad – that's all. Start by practising following the trail of your mum or dad in the back garden or along a well-used track in a nearby wood or park. The beach is the best place to learn as the tracks can be seen very easily in the soft sand.

The first thing to do is to ask Mum and Dad to walk along for a few metres side by side. When they have done this you press one of the small sticks into the ground close to the first visible print where they began walking, then tear off a small piece of newspaper to make a flag as shown. Repeat this along the trail as you follow the tracks and soon you will begin to see a pattern appear. In both cases the distance between each set of prints will be about the same. On closer examination you may notice that Dad's prints will seem to be a lot deeper than Mum's, because he is probably heavier and bigger than her, and Mum's prints will be much closer than Dad's, because Mum does not stride out as far as Dad.

So in just a few minutes you are already beginning to work like a professional tracker.

Once you can easily recognize walking prints ask your parents to try running, and mark out as before.

If someone is walking along casually, they tend to place the heel of the foot down on the ground first and transfer the weight of the body on to the toe as they move forward. In doing this they press most of their weight down on the heel so the heel imprint will be much deeper than that of the toes.

When running it is the toes that touch the ground first and as the foot leaves the ground, it spurts backwards. So when walking the back edge of the heel is shown clearly. When running, it is the leading edge of the toes that is shown clearly.

So, in a matter of seconds you as the tracker can tell if the trail you are following is a running or walking one, and by placing your marker flags alongside the trail you can stand back and instantly see where the trail goes.

Human footprints

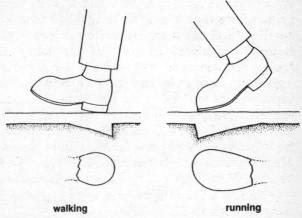

walking   running

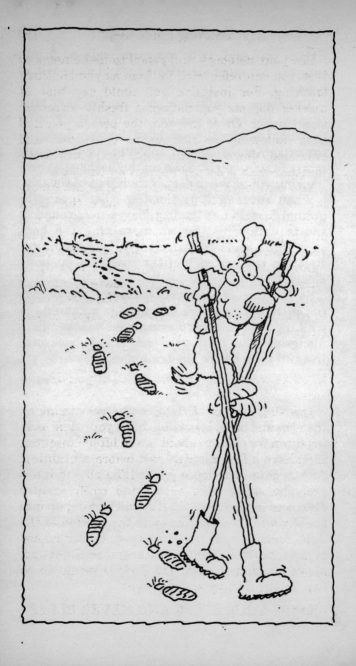

Use your notebook and pencil to make notes so that you can refer back to them as you continue tracking. For instance, you could say that at marker flag six you noticed a freshly discarded sweet paper. Or at flag ten, the person you had been following seemed to have stopped and crouched down as the two footprints were together with a deeper imprint on the toes.

You may even suddenly find the prints breaking into a trot then back into a walk, then back into a trot. So you can assume that the person is either jogging and walking, or trying to confuse you, especially if they know that they are being followed. It could be that they are late and in a hurry to get back home so they have to run and walk to make up time. Whatever the case it is up to you, the tracker, to interpret the signs. A good tip is to use the old Army rule.

IF IN DOUBT, STEP OUT

In other words, do not blunder on if you are not sure . . . STOP and rethink.

Tracking for long periods can be very tiring on the eyes and back. If possible limit your time looking down for signs to about ten to fifteen minutes, then have a few minutes' rest before continuing. As you gain experience you will be able to interpret the signs more easily and cover greater distances in a quicker time. Avoid looking up into the sky and then back down to the ground as the light contrast will tire your eyes. Under no circumstances look directly into bright sunlight and, above all, do not rush. Tracking is meant to be fun. In the army you are taught

KNOW YOUR STUFF AND NEVER BLUFF

The difficult stuff

Once you are satisfied that you can follow a simple walking trail ask your parents to try some sideways steps or run backwards. Study the prints and see how they differ from the others.

Walking sideways, for instance, means that you have to place the whole of your foot down on the ground. Running backwards means that your legs quickly become tired. Both are very difficult to do over long distances because they are unnatural movements. So walking on the outside edge of your feet, attempting to tiptoe, or any other odd movement such as hopping or skipping only helps the tracker. What does confuse the tracker is if the person whose trail he/she is following is simply walking along casually. It can then be very difficult for the tracker to interpret any sign changes.

Look with your ears; hear with your eyes

When I was living with the Aborigines in Australia and practising my tracking, they used to tell me to look with my ears, and hear with my eyes. In other words to use my senses in two ways. For instance, though I could see someone walking way in the distance, because they were too far away for me to hear them, I was to use my eyes as my ears and imagine the sound they made as they walked.

You too can practise this skill and you don't have to go all the way to Australia to learn it.

Take a trip to the local park or sit outside your
front gate and wait for someone to come along.
When they get near to you, close your eyes and
see if you can match a sound in your head to the
one they make as they pass by. Another excellent
way to learn to put sounds to signs is to get your
friend to walk, run, jump or whatever close by you
and note the different noises.

Why do you do this? Well, remember I said
earlier that sometimes people try to confuse the
tracker by running backwards, sideways, on tiptoe, etc. But in so doing they unintentionally alter
the sign left on the ground so when you, the
tracker, come along you can immediately interpret these changes in signs.

Early in the morning is the best time to go
tracking as the sun's shadows do not confuse you
and the heat of the day will not have dried up any
tracks left, such as splashes of water on leaves
as the animals move around the undergrowth.
Many animals lie up during the day, seeking food
in the early hours of the morning or as the sun
sets. This way they get lots of moisture from the
cooling foliage and digest their last meal. In very
hot places almost all living things, including
people, rest up during the day's intense heat and
tracking is made difficult with the shimmering
ground and murky dust.

The ability to track well can, as I have said
earlier, help save lives. More than once I have
followed the trail of a wild animal in the bush and
it has led me to precious drinking water. Out
there my life depended on my tracking skills. For
you it is a hobby but it could so easily save your
life too in an emergency.

11

Against all odds: true survival stories

Because this book is not only about planning and preparing your first outdoor adventures but also how to stay alive in an emergency, I have included in this chapter four true stories in which young people found themselves in real survival situations. All the stories are real, but I have changed the names and locations.

Car crash in the snow

Fourteen-year-old Hamish McGregor felt the first warm droplets of blood fall on to his aching arm as he lay trapped in the tangled metal of the upturned landrover.

Earlier that day he and his father had been doing a little shopping in Glasgow and were now returning to their hill farm high in the Scottish mountains. It was the end of January and already there was a deep fall of snow covering the hills.

Turning off the main road up the long winding track to the farm, the Landrover suddenly spun out of control on a sharp bend, sending the vehicle and its two occupants hurtling down into a nearby brook.

A good hour passed before young Hamish came

to. His unconscious father hung upside down in his seat belt with a deep gash in his forehead, and the whole vehicle smelt heavily of petrol.

Hamish managed to free himself and crawled out of the vehicle. His first thoughts were for his dad and, ignoring the pain in his left arm, he tried to free him and pull him clear. As he worked, fresh snow was falling hard and after the noise of the accident the glen took on an eerie silence as the blanket of snow enshrouded everything. With a great deal of effort and pain, Hamish finally managed to free his father, drag him clear of the vehicle and lay him down gently in the snow.

Quickly he set about trying to stop the flow of blood from his dad's head wound by removing his tie and making an improvised bandage. After repeatedly trying to wake his dad, he removed his own coat and laid it gently over him to protect him from the falling snow.

Hamish's body hurt all over. He had taken a nasty knock on the head, and suffered a severe gash to his left arm.

Inside the Landrover he found a pack of old plastic feed bags. Quickly he tore these into strips and used them to bandage up his injuries. He cut a hole in one of them, and then slipped it over his shoulder to make an improvised jacket.

At this stage exhaustion took over his body and he collapsed in the snow alongside his father. Some time later he heard a long, low moan and woke with a start. His left arm now throbbed painfully and the biting cold tore at his limbs. Crawling over to his father he gently laid a hand on his injured head. 'Don't worry, Dad,' he said. 'I'll get help. Can you hold on?'

Mr McGregor nodded and waved his son off, then fell back into unconsciousness. Hamish placed the rest of the plastic bags over his dad for protection and struggled back up the hill.

Slipping and sliding, he eventually made it back to the track and, fighting to stay awake, turned to walk the three miles to the farm. He was unaware that his arm was broken, that he had a head wound that needed twenty stitches and also had a deep gash on his ankle. Some three hours later he stumbled through the front door of the farm to raise the alarm.

The rescue services and ambulance were immediately alerted by Mrs McGregor but, because of the exceptionally bad weather, it was to be almost two hours before the rescue party eventually managed to reach the wreck. Mr McGregor had broken ribs, a severe head wound, a broken arm and massive bruising, not to mention hypothermia. Only the quick thinking and unselfishness of his fourteen-year-old son had saved his life.

In conditions described as the worst for half a century and suffering from shock, exposure and severe injuries, young Hamish McGregor managed to survive the accident, and save not only his own life but that of his father.

Today Hamish and his parents still work the hill farm, but none of them will forget that cold winter's day.

Trapped below ground

'Zero, this is One Alpha, do you copy? Over.'

'One Alpha, go ahead. Over.'

'Zero, we have reached the old mine shaft and will begin rescue procedure immediately.'

'Roger, One Alpha, the ambulance is on its way. Keep us informed. Over.'

More than 35 metres below ground, trapped in an old disused mineshaft twelve-year-old Kathy Smith lay conscious, but half submerged in freezing, murky water.

Above her, a team of rescuers was working frantically against the clock trying to get Kathy out as quickly as possible.

'What's the latest on the weather,' called the team leader to the police officer standing by the radio.

'Not good, I'm afraid. Met office warns of a cold front closing in and heavy rain within the hour.'

By the old mine shaft one of the rescuers was busy lowering a microphone and battery torch down to the trapped girl below. 'Get that plastic covering up and around the entrance as quickly as you can, lads,' called the rescue leader. 'Let's hope that there's no underground stream running into the shaft. What do you think, Doctor? If she is alive, what are her chances of surviving?'

'Don't really know,' replied the doctor. 'Until we can get that light and microphone down we can only guess. My main concern is debris falling down on top of her, so tell your boys to take care.'

Walking home from school with her friend Sherry, across waste land beside a disused col-

liery in a West Yorkshire mining village, Kathy
suddenly plummeted down an old air shaft. The
opening was not much more than half a metre in
diameter, but over the years the edges had broken
away and grass and other common weeds had
grown over the now rotted metal cover. Repeatedly Sherry called out to her friend but got no
reply. Not wanting to waste time, she ran off to
seek help.

By a stroke of good luck, Kathy's descent into
the murky depths of the mine shaft came to a
sudden halt at the water level as her right
shoulder became trapped against the narrow
shaft walls.

Shaken, but not physically hurt other than a
few bruises, Kathy very bravely took stock of the
situation and realized that if she were to free her
shoulder she would slide down even further.

She forced herself to keep calm and trust Sherry
to do the sensible thing. Patiently, she settled
down to wait for rescue.

After what seemed an age, she heard noises
above her, and realized that help had arrived.

As she hung there small stones and clumps of
earth began to fall around her shoulders and
head. This scared Kathy and she called out to the
rescue team to take care as the loose debris was
making it difficult for her to lift her head.

After what seemed an eternity, a rope holding
the microphone and torch gently bumped against
her head. With one arm free she took hold and
gave it a firm tug.

A strong but soothing male voice suddenly came
from the microphone. 'Steady now, Kathy. We
don't want the sides of the shaft falling on your

head. If you can, take the microphone in your hand and, when I tell you, slowly tell me if you are injured, and if you can move your arms and legs. Speak now.'

Kathy quickly explained her situation and the rescue leader then told her to untie the microphone so that he could pull up the rope and send down a protective hat to guard her head.

The helmet appeared and, using one arm, Kathy quickly untied it from the rope, put it on, and managed to fasten the end of the rope around her waist. All the time the gentle male voice was giving her lots of encouragement.

In the pitch blackness young Kathy's strength was beginning to fade and she repeatedly asked to speak to her parents who had to be brought from work.

Eventually they arrived and Kathy began sobbing as she talked to them but did not become hysterical. Meanwhile, unknown to Kathy, special machinery had to be fetched to dig a parallel shaft as the rescuers felt that any attempt to try and pull her out could end up burying her alive.

For the rest of the day and most of the night the rescue team frantically worked at digging the parallel shaft and after twelve hours of continuous hard work they eventually managed to break through and rescue Kathy.

Throughout the whole ordeal Kathy Smith remained calm and in full control of her emotions. Not able to tell whether it was day or night, hanging suspended, wedged in a deep narrow shaft by one of her shoulders, with the lower half of her body submerged in freezing, smelly water, she was able to speak calmly to her parents and rescuers as she waited patiently.

Kathy refused to give in. At no time did she panic. When eventually she was rescued and brought to the surface, she was found to have suffered a broken nose, fractured ankle, a dislocated shoulder, and slight rope burns to her body.

Today, Kathy is a lovely young teenager with no physical or mental scars; only a fading memory of that terrible ordeal when her best friend Sherry ran to fetch help and saved her life.

Coral island castaway

The first indication that something was wong was when he tried to sit up. Bruised and sore and badly burnt from the hot tropical sun, thirteen-year-old Peter Davies had lain washed up on a remote coral island off the east coast of Africa for two days before he began to regain consciousness.

Slowly the warm sun began to revive him, his throat felt sore and dry, and his nostrils twitched as he smelt the salt in the hot sand and decaying seaweed around him.

Peter had been on holiday in Mombasa, Kenya, staying with friends of his parents. Five days before he had decided to do a little inshore dinghy sailing and was happily pottering about amongst the reefs when a school of dolphins began playing around beneath his boat.

The sea was reasonably calm, with a slight breeze blowing, and the surrounding water was crystal clear. Watching the dolphins at play Peter became completely immersed in their antics and

failed to notice his boat drifting further and
further away from the mainland. Suddenly there
was a shattering clap of thunder – immediately
above him, it seemed – and seconds later he
found himself being thrown around in the dinghy
as the strong tide pulled him into the surging
waters of the main coral reef.

Completely unprepared, Peter was thrown into
the turbulent waters as the boat capsized. Unable
to right the boat, he clung on desperately to a
trailing line as the crashing waves tried to tear
him free. All around him the storm raged and in
what seemed just a few seconds the sea became a
boiling inferno.

For two whole days Peter battled to survive and
fought for his life clinging to the shattered hull of
the dinghy. Eventually the storm subsided, but
not before the small boat had broken up on the
pounding reef.

Through sheer determination Peter was able to
drag himself ashore over the razor-sharp coral.
He collapsed on a small sandy beach, completely
exhausted, and there he lay for two days and
nights, unconscious, until thirst and hunger
eventually woke him.

Whilst the storm raged, a rescue party had been
out searching for Peter. They did not hold out
much hope of finding him alive as they had found
pieces of his dinghy drifting amongst the shark-
infested coral reef. Peter, of course, was very
much alive and when he slowly began to regain
consciousness he realized that if he was to survive
and be rescued he had to start looking for
something to drink and eat, build a shelter and
put out marker signals to help his rescuers.

Nearby on the beach were half a dozen coconut trees laden with fresh fruit. During the storm some had been blown down. These coconuts gave Peter his first drink and meal for five days.

During the day he sheltered beneath the shade of the trees and at night to keep warm he covered himself in dry sand, seaweed and palm fronds. He cleaned out all the grazes and cuts he had received whilst being tossed about on the sharp coral, using fresh sea water to wash them, and wrapping them in seaweed. (He had read somewhere in one of his school books that seaweed was rich in iodine.)

To help his rescuers spot him from the air he set out large shells and debris to form the international distress signal S. O. S.

For the next few days young Peter scratched and rummaged around trying to stay alive, but, weak from exposure and slowly becoming dehydrated, his spirits began to fall. On the morning of his sixth day on the small island he awoke to the sound of falling rain. Quickly he washed himself and his clothing in the fresh water, sat beneath the coconut tree for shelter and began to pray as tears streamed down his face.

Later that evening the rain stopped and Peter got up to take yet another walk around the island. As he rounded a sand bar he stopped dead in his tracks. There, just a couple of hundred metres away, a group of local fishermen were busy winding in nets. He could hardly contain himself and ran towards the fishermen waving his hands in the air, shouting, 'I'm here, help me.'

Two days later the fishermen sailed into

Mombasa harbour and safely delivered Peter to
the local hospital.

Thirteen-year-old Peter Davis survived because
he refused to die. Shipwrecked and at sea, drifting
around in shark-infested waters, he hung on to
life, and when he eventually found himself
washed ashore he quickly organized his survival.
In his last moments of despair he turned to prayer
for guidance as many thousands of people in
similar survival situations have done before him.
Survival isn't just about lighting fires, building
shelters, and finding food, it is also about finding
yourself. Without the will to survive you will die.
It is as simple as that.

Lost in the mist

Petra Morgan was a sensible girl. She knew that
if she did not remain calm and take control of the
situation she and her best friend Helen would
soon die.

Both girls had been out walking with a party of
friends across the bleak Welsh mountains late
one autumn morning. The weather had been fine
with a slight ground mist in the valley and a soft
fall of fresh snow high on the mountain tops.

Laughing and giggling, they strolled along at
the rear as the main party climbed higher into
the hills. Gradually the two girls began to fall
further and further behind and eventually they
lost sight of the others altogether. But as the
weather ahead was still good this did not alarm
them, and both seemed oblivious to the change

taking place down below in the valley. The mist
had thickened considerably since they began, and
had already started creeping silently up,
engulfing the hills behind the two girls as it did
so, and causing a sudden drop in temperature.
Before long Helen and Petra felt the chilled air
and decided to stop and put on some extra warm
clothing.

Every member of the party had been instructed
to bring with them a rucksack containing a set of
waterproofs, a spare sweater, a flask containing a
hot drink, sandwiches, a whistle, torch and
compass.

A sense of urgency now gripped the two girls as
they became aware of the quickening weather
change – in just a few minutes the silent, grey
mist completely enshrouded the hills. Panic
swept over them and they began running and
calling to the others ahead, but after half an hour
of continuous shouting and scrambling around in
the swirling, thickening mist, they were forced to
stop and rest. Physically exhausted, scared, and
with their throats sore from shouting, they
huddled together for comfort.

Petra had been out walking many times and
was much fitter than Helen and, as this was her
friend's first time in the hills, she quickly realized
that she must take charge of the situation. The
first thing was to put on their waterproofs and
spare clothing, and (to help gain control of their
fears) have a warm drink. Petra knew the others
would be searching for them and to blunder
further into the mist would be unwise. It would be
better to rest and sit it out, giving the main party
time to find them.

After a quick drink of hot coffee Petra asked Helen to take her whistle from the pack and quickly explained about the international distress call signal.

'We will take it in turns,' she said, 'ten minutes each. We blow six five-second blasts every minute or so and if they hear us they will reply with three long blasts. Remember though,' she warned Helen, 'it is important that we remain where we are even when we know they have heard us. We let them come to us.'

They began signalling, and after each series of blasts they listened with ears strained for the reply – but there was none.

By now almost six hours had passed since they first became separated from the main party and, to add to their danger, the mist was beginning to turn into a freezing drizzle. If Petra and Helen did not get down off the mountain soon they would die from hypothermia.

Unknown to both girls, the wheels of rescue had already been put into operation. The group leader, realizing what had happened, had sent a party down into the valley to warn the mountain rescue team whilst he and the remainder continued the search.

Meanwhile Helen's stamina was beginning to ebb away in the chilling mist and drizzle, and already she was weak from hunger and cold. All she wanted to do was to lie down and go to sleep. Petra recognized this as being an advanced stage of hypothermia and began to hold Helen closer so that the warmth from her body would help keep Helen warm. Using her own rucksack she tipped out all its contents and pushed Helen's feet inside, wrapping them in her spare sweater. She also made her friend sit on the other rucksack to protect her from the damp earth.

A survival trick she had learnt from her father was to take off her waterproof jacket and drape this across the shoulders like a cape. 'This way,' he had said, 'it helps to keep in the heat better. It traps the air. Tight clothing restricts the air flow.'

To make sure that Helen did not drift off into a sleep Petra looked around for and found a nearby sheltered spot behind a large rock. She made Helen sit there with her back against hers and feet drawn up close. This ensured a strong physical body contact that is very important to anyone suffering from hypothermia. It made Helen aware and reassured her that someone was close at all times.

Sitting there back to back, Petra protected Helen from some of the biting wind and as she did so, her Dad's voice drifted into her mind. 'Remember' he had said, 'the three main killers out there in the wilds are the cold, wet and wind. If you are caught out, to stay alive it is important that you seek protection as soon as possible.'

As the day wore on and night began to fall the drizzle continued. Neither girl wore a watch so they had no idea what time of day it was, but Petra realized that as darkness fell any chance of rescue before morning would be very slim and if they were to sit there feeling sorry for themsleves both of them would probably die.

Taking occasional sips of coffee, telling jokes, singing the latest hits, the two girls continued to comfort each other throughout the night. Petra's quick thinking had helped to restore some of

Helen's confidence, and they now took it in turn to use the whistle. As they huddled together they chatted and made up games until eventually, completely exhausted, they both fell asleep.

It was Helen who stirred first, shaking off the stiffness of the night. 'Listen,' she said, shaking Petra awake. 'Listen, I can hear someone calling.'

Scrambling to their feet they began to shout and whistle in the direction of the voices. 'Over here. We're over here. Help.' Helen began waving her pack above her head.

It was early morning and the thick mountain mist had drifted away, leaving a thin covering of light snow. Soon a familiar shape came over the ridge close to them. It was the party leader. Gathering up their belongings and stuffing them into their packs they dashed to meet him. Seconds later, with tears streaming down their faces, they were surrounded by the rest of the rescue team.

A few days later, during school assembly, the headmistress firstly read out a stern warning to everyone about the dangers ever-present on such adventures and how lack of discipline can easily bring about a disaster. Then she read out a bravery citation to both the girls from the mountain rescue leader. Petra in particular was praised. 'Her quick thinking and level headedness,' he said, 'had almost certainly saved Helen's and her own life.'

Because the two girls managed to stay calm and not panic, both survived.

Two months later, on the same mountain, an inexperienced adult walker died of hypothermia.